T0064120

From a Caterpillar Into a Butterfly

From a Caterpillar Into a Butterfly

Winnie L.B.Toh

PARTRIDGE
A Penguin Random House Company

ISBN: Hardcover 978-1-4828-2851-1
Softcover 978-1-4828-2850-4
eBook 978-1-4828-2852-8

Print information available on the last page.

To order additional copies of this book, contact
Toll Free 800 101 2657 (Singapore)
Toll Free 1 800 81 7340 (Malaysia)
orders.singapore@partridgepublishing.com

www.partridgepublishing.com/singapore

DEDICATED TO:

WARMEST REGARDS,

PRAISE AND COMMENTS

"No matter how far you have wandered, how broken your life is, or how shattered your dreams are, Jesus' love can grip and transform you beyond your wildest imagination. He has demonstrated this in Winnie's life and He can do so uniquely in yours too! The journey may be different but His grace and power is just as real."

-Pastor Ng Kok Aun
Georgetown Baptist Church (GBC)

"I personally witness the ordeal you went through. Thank God you persisted in your faith believing that Jesus will set you free. Your experience written down in words are real. All honour & glory be to our Almighty God!"

– Sylvester Phan,
Church Senior *Ipoh Lutheran Church*

"Thank you for sharing your testimony with the Cell group tonight. It was truely unique." *via sms*

– Chan Chee Kong, Cell Group Leader
Georgetown Baptist Church

"Winnie is really good in expressing her emotions into her writing Every chapter I read, I can feel the emotional struggles that she was going through. I believe this book can bring more people closer to God."

– Nickey Teoh, Publishing Director
of The Inspiration Hub

It has been wonderful to see God working in your life as we study His life giving word together this year in Bible Study Fellowship (BSF). So keep your eyes fixed on Jesus at all times and trust in Him with all your heart. His grace will be sufficient for you.

– Jayanthi Dhanaraj BSF Group Leader

This book deserves to be shared worldwide. The thoughts are so amazing and so realistic to read. I paused and I imagine about your life experiences. I know that you're not counting with the investment that you made and the possible sales that you might get. It's clear to me that your intention is to share your thoughts to the world as being a good Christian.

– Joel Araneta
SENIOR Publishing Consultant
Partridge Singapore

"I believe in your experience. It may be weird but it is real."

– Ricky Soo, Internet Business Developer

"My son enjoys reading your story. He is looking forward to reading your next scripts."

– Benjamin Sim, Ipoh

"The fact that Winnie would want to use her resources (time, money and effort) to reach those who have similar needs reveals that this Jesus must be really special."

– Hannah Tan, GBC

"I see it as examples and as warnings for us.. in the hope that every reader will come to their senses and escape from the trap of the devil.."

– Grace Chew, GBC

"It is interesting as what I have heard during your sharing in CG, it will encourage many especially those unbelief for their faith in Christ. Indeed, The Lord has guided and used your testimony to reach those unbelief. May The Lord bless your journey with Him abundantly!

- Su Anne, Cell Group member, GBC

“If we love one another, all men will know that you are my disciples.”.

- John 1 3:35

Dedicated to

JESUS AND HIS DISCIPLES

Pastor Lai (a dedicated Pastor who spent the most time helping me go through my ordeal) • Pastor Michel Wright (who taught me about the Word of God) • Pastor David (who travelled all the way from Ipoh to visit me and prayed for me) • Christine Oon (Thank you for being so supportive. I will always remember you teaching me my first Christian song 'Sing Hallelujah to the Lord') • Benjamin Sim (The person who led me to accept Christ overnight via sms. I have never regretted my decision till this very day.) • Rosamund (Thank you for the lovely cream puffs, all the way from Ipoh) • Mr Phan (who prayed for me over the phone and follow-up with me regularly) • Madam Koay from Ipoh (Although you do not know me, I am touched and blessed that you willingly spent your precious time visiting me just to share your testimony) • Stephen Tong (who introduced me Pastor Michel) • Kimara Tong (who taught me the definition of the word 'rebuke' over the phone) • Aaron Toh (Thank you for connecting me to DUMC when I was looking for assistance in K.L.) • Dr. Chia from Adventist Hospital (who made a special appointment with me to pray for me during patients hour) • DUMC Church Cell Group • Ricky Soo (Thank you for referring me to a Pastor in KL and for your relentless sup- portive in Facebook) • Wen Wong (Thank you for your encourage- ment in Facebook) • My facebook Christian friends (Thank you for the supportive posts)

May all your names appear in the book of Heaven.

Dedicated to

NON-CHRISTIAN FRIENDS AND RELATIVES

Max, my hubby (who is not against me embracing Christianity after witnessing all that I had gone through) • My mum (who stoodby me throughout the ordeal and tried finding countless ways to help me out of my ordeal.) • My sister-in-law Saw June (who brought me to explore special healing) • My cousin (who made Old Wives Tale healing medicine for the assumed sicknesses) • My Aunts (who are understanding and considerate despite my unexpected conversion to Christianity) • Some of the sisters from Tzu Chi Organisation Miss Khor (my business partner who gave me the blessing in my journey of accepting Christ) • My students (Thank you for being considerable and for allowing me to cancel the classes)

JESUS

"Not to us, O Lord, not to us but to your name be the glory..."

– Psalm 115:1

Lord, I humbly come before You and ask for Your for giveness should I have esteemed myself more than I should in this book (whether in my writings or pictures). Please for give me if I have unintentionally positioned Your disciples above You. Even though I am grateful for all that they have done, we are merely Your vessels and we long to bring honour to Your name. Help us to love one another and live our lives in humility before You. All glor y goes to our Lord Jesus Christ!

Contents

FOREWORD

The journey of any Christian is an important imprint in our journey of destiny. Winnie has expressed her steps in this journey and I believe it will help anyone reading this to realize how important people are in our lives and as we partake this journey God sends his human "angels" to assist. Love the "title", read and be blessed.

- Pastor Michel Wright
Kingdom Transformation Sanctuary -
ISAAC, Kuala Lumpur

ACKNOWLEDGEMENTS

I am indebted to our Lord Jesus Christ. It was God at work behind the scene. You are my inspiration for this project. Thank You, Father, for Your saving grace and the motivation to write this book. Your ministry is nationwide and miraculous. I still remember receiving my salvation from Ipoh and how my book-writing journey began in Ipoh. The assistance I received as I was going through my ordeal came all the way from siblings in Christ in Kuala Lumpur. Coincidently, I was also connected to Inspiration Hub from Kuala Lumpur to further develop this book. A special word of thanks goes to Nickey Teoh and editorial team members Hazel Saw and Rebecca Liew for your empowering words which help to take the book to the next level.

My deepest gratitude goes to Benjamin Sim from Ipoh for helping me transport the scripts to and fro between Penang and Ipoh throughout the year. Thank you for being supportive in helping me to source for information and giving constructive opinions. You are a great mentor to me. Each time you come to Penang, it stirred me to make progress for the book. Not forgetting my first stage editor Mr Phan from Ipoh for editing the book for me. You have a pure heart to do God's work and thank you for your priceless work. You are the answer to my prayer. Shortly after I made the decision to write this book, God instantly provided me resources I needed from Ipoh. Words cannot express how grateful I am to you. Thank you for your uplifting words in times when I was really down and when I almost gave up this project in halfway through. It seemed as though God had sent you to energize me at the right time. God did not foresake me when I needed comfort the most. He connected me to Hwee Tiang, my cell group

member to be my faithful listener. Thanks to Susan and Josephine Lo for your prayers during the period when my book-writing project was left idle. I remembered attending a very inspiring talk at Jo's place. It was as though the Lord was sending a reminder to me to go back to the project when the project was stagnant for three months.

To the team of creative graphic designers--Sze Yan, Adrian and Hooi Dic-Syen--a big thank you for your amazing artwork. A special thanks to Sze Yan for delivering your work on time. Thanks to Hannah Tan from GBC for your invaluable input and relevant suggestions of the Bible verses. To my Masterlife study partner Mew Leng, thank you for believing in my testimony. You are the only person who put yourself in my shoes and told me that you could not imagine yourself going through my ordeal. To my beloved husband, Max Loh, thank you for the interesting suggestions of the graphic design from an architect point of view. You are an answer to my prayer financially. I remembered once after I paid the money for developing the book, our insurance consultant refunded an amount of money very closed to the figure I paid in my name. You did not object to it. Instead, you offered to sponsor the printing of the books if needed.

Thanks to an International Publishing company which persistently approached me from the early stage of my book-writing project until the final stage. Each time when I heard from them, it motivated me to make progress for the book. And finally, I did sign up as I took it as God's open door for the project to go worldwide.

Thanks to a new team members Joel Araneta, Shelly Edmunds and Chris Lodovice for taking the book to the next level.

Last but not least, Thank you Jesus again. You are the first and the last. Your provision is superfluous and more than what I asked for!

AUTHOR'S NOTE

I swore I would never again publish another book in my life. But I changed my mind when I did the sinners prayer. If I were to choose to write a book that benefits me most, I could have chosen to write another book which is related to my previous book's category. I am better off investing my time in writing a book which has more promising sales. Nonetheless, I have chosen to write a Christian book. The sincerity of my heart for Christ is clearly attested here.

This book is written as an expression of my love to Jesus, as a token of appreciation to my Christian friends who had journeyed and helped me through my ordeal as well as to share my personal encounter with the True Living God with others. As a young Christian, I am still very new to writing a Christian book. No matter how hard it is to produce this book, I will surge ahead. I have faith that in Christ, all things are possible.

Like many, I had no interest in knowing Christ before. I never expected myself to wake up from my sleep one day realising that I am already a Christian. In many of my old profile documents, my religion is still recorded as a Buddhist. It was a rapid conversion for me indeed. The metamorphosis that I went through can be likened to the life cycle of a butterfly Metamorphosis which takes approximately 6-8 weeks to complete.

If you ever wonder how it feels like going through a metamorphosis, transforming from a caterpillar into a butterfly, read on and experience this with me. I invite you to put your feelings into it when reading and

join me on this journey of metamorphosis of drastic change in my spiritual encounter.

If you ever wonder how it feels like going through a metamorphosis, transforming from a caterpillar into a butterfly, read on and

This book is written as a gift to those who are open to the Gospel. I am sharing the truth that Jesus has set me free. To other young Christians, be encouraged. If it is possible for me to start life over with Christ, so can you!

PREFACE

This book "From a Caterpillar into a Butterfly" is a non-fiction novel, in attempt of making it reader-friendly to non-Christians. Most of the scripture references are recorded as footnotes in each chapter as references for believers of Christ. When I was a new believer, I love to hear testimonies of how other believers come to accept Christ in their lives. So I thought this book would also help those who are seeking for an answer as well as new believers to build up their faith in Jesus.

To my non-Christian friends who did not witness my ordeal, it might appear to you that I betrayed my previous religion. As it is difficult for me to recite the same story to everyone, I decided to write it down. My story is lengthy enough to be compiled into a book. Some parts of the story might stretch credulity of the unbelievers. Nonetheless, I have tried to record the exact dates and time by tracing my previous SMS and Facebook wall posts. I would like to thank those who believed in my story.

Since I accepted Christ on 11.11.2009, I have always wanted to share my testimony with others. However, I was not able to divulge much of the story during the time of my ordeal. Every time when I tried recalling the ordeal, I felt sick. Now that almost two years have gone by, I felt that it is time for me to come out into the open and share this chapter

Some parts of the story might stretch credulity of the unbelievers. Nonetheless, I have tried to record the exact dates and time by tracing my previous sms and facebook wall posts.

of my life and share it with others. I still have vivid flashback of the ordeal till this very day.

The story came about in October 2009 when I participated in a nationwide beauty pageant contest (for mothers), which is also known as "From a Caterpillar to a Butterfly". The winner will be crowned with the title 'Angel'. In this contest, the organiser intended to prove their capability in making everyone beautiful from the inside out. So they conducted a ten-hour spiritual training which was a compulsory module for all contestants in the beauty contest. During the spiritual training, we were hypnotized and brought to a so-called "heaven" and had visualisation of the year 2012. I experience spiritual death amid the transformation and Jesus came as my Saviour at the right time. I accepted Christ overnight via an SMS from a Christian friend. Accepting Jesus was my only hope to coming back alive spiritually.

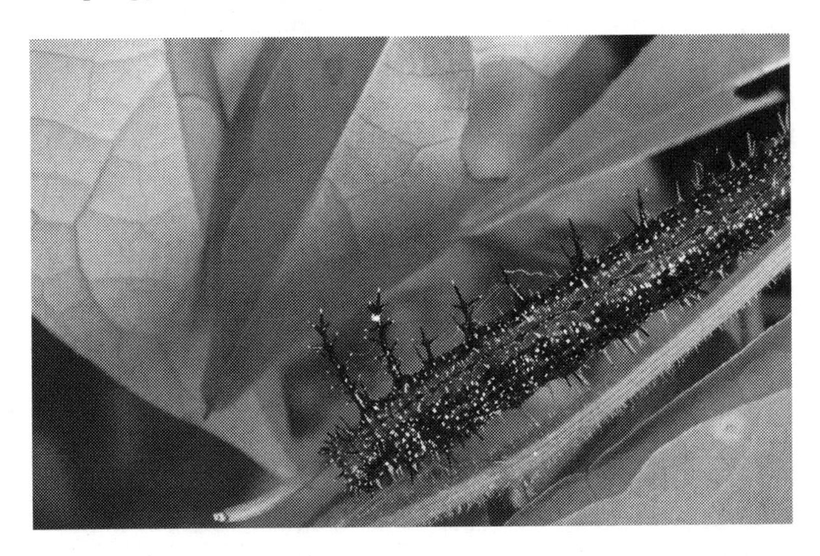

I am a child of God now. My story depicts the process of transformation and the rebirth of a new spirit in Christ I experienced,

which reflected the title of this book 'From A Caterpillar into A Butterfly".

Find out how this beauty contest had brought about a metamorphosis journey in my life from a caterpillar to a butterfly, not the Butterfly the beauty contest's organiser intended for me to become but the butterfly that God has made me to be.

I am a child of God now. My story depicts the process of transformation and the rebirth of a new spirit in Christ I experienced, which reflected the title of this book 'From A Caterpillar into A Butterfly".

TRANSFORMATION PROCESS:

Egg → Caterpillar → Pupa → Butterfly

The Death of My Old Self and The Rebirth of A New Life in Christ...

PURCHASED BY THE LAMB OF GOD

"Since when have you been a converted Christian, Winnie? I thought you are a religious Buddhist."

I have many friends who asked me this question. For those who knew me well, I was indeed a very religious Buddhist who visited the Buddhist temples regularly. What made me gave up on everything that I have been so familiar with without giving it a second thought and proceed on to start a new life with Christ? The answer is simple. If it was not Jesus who saved my life in a near death experience (being tormented by Satan), I would have never changed my religion.

In the past, I was a staunch Buddhist, one who wore a black robe[1] chanting before the statue of Buddha. I was even given two passports to bring with me in my casket when I pass on, and with these passports, I can have the privilege to be at the 'priority lane' when queuing up to enter the heaven's door.

I thought I have secured myself with two passports to heaven given by my previous religion.

---

[1] A black robe(hai-qing) is supposed to be worn by the decedent who has taken the Buddhist vow(san gui yi) during lifetime on the funeral day in the casket and the passports must be buried together so that the Buddhist can enter the heaven after life.

I had put much effort and gone that far but I decided to foresake everything and start my spiritual life all over again from scratch with Jesus. Yes, I had been converted to Christianity and am purchased by the blood of the Lamb overnight[1]. There is no turning back. The die is cast.

---

1 2 Corinthians 5:17 Therefore, if anyone is in Christ, the new creation has come: The old has gone, the new is here!

If Jesus hadn't saved my life in a near death experience (being tormented by Satan), I would have never ever changed my religion.

AND HOW DID IT HAPPEN?

So how did it all happen? Let me relive the moment to share this story..

It all began with my visit to a beauty salon for a facial treatment one day. I overheard a conversation going on between the therapists in the beauty salon encouraging their manager to take part in a Beauty Pageant Contest. The manager said she had given it a thought for the last two weeks. However, she met with a road accident and it put her off from going foward with it. I supposed she is a Christian and to her, the accident was a blessing in disguise.

"What is it? What is it?" Out of curiosity, I budged into the conversation.

"It's a Beauty Pageant Contest for the married women. Oh Winnie, are you interested? If you are, I can find out the contact information for you. We saw the ad in the Chinese newspapers quite some time ago." one of the therapists replied.

"Beauty Pageant Contest? I have never participated one in my life. Don't think I am qualified. Perish the thought!" I thought to myself.

"Why not Winnie and Priscilla join this together?" the therapist asked.

"Oh no! I just had an accident. Moreover, this Beauty Pageant Contest is about to begin training soon. The trainers will be training the contestants to achieve perfection, becoming the ideal women from the inside out. Which means anyone can be a part of this contest regardless of size of looks. It sounded to me that it is indeed for people who are still not very satisfied with themselves. I am already satisfied. I do not see the need of making anymore improvements. Besides, I am very tied down with work." Priscilla replied.

"O.K. Winnie. We'll get the necessary information for you then." one of the therapists replied.

I did not give much thought to it as I was not exactly desperate. to be part of the Beauty Pageant Contest. The only reason I was interested during that time was because I was curious.

A few days later, I received a phone call from one of the therapists from the beauty parlour. She gave me the organiser's contact number.

"Try calling the organiser to ask for more information, Winnie. I think the sign-ups are still open. They are still advertising it." she said.

The words lingered in my mind. Should I? Or don't bother?

I had some free time. Prompted by curiosity, I started dialling the organiser's numbers for enquiry.

"Do come and attend our talk at Evergreen Laurel Hotel. tomorrow. And don't forget to buy the Chinese newspapers tomorrow for further information." the organiser said.

"But I am giving tuition classes all the way until 4:30p.m. Your talk will end at 5 p.m." I protested hesitantly.

"That's alright. Just turn up after you have finished your tuition classes. I'll be waiting for you." the organiser assured me.

I thought I would better get a copy of the newspapers and find out what was it all about before attending the talk at Evergreen Laurel Hotel.

I managed to attain the newspapers on Saturday morning. Flipping through the pages, something caught my attention immediately. There it was--A half-page advertisement. It was a nationwide beauty pageant contest (for mothers). There is also another name for it i.e. from a caterpillar to a butterfly. The winner will be crowned with the title 'Angel God'. It was a distinguished beauty pageant contest in the sense that the focus was not only on the physical beauty of the contestants but also the internal beauty. What was unique was that they provided trainers to groom and to train up the contestants who took part in the contest.

"O.K. I am not going to cancel my tuition classes for the talk. Just let it be. If I can make it, I will be there. Otherwise, just forget it!" Convincingly I told myself.

By the time everything finished it was already 4:30p.m. I was hesitant whether I should still go.

The organiser said she would wait for me. Have I sounded like I have promised her to be there? May be I should just go and take a look at the event.

Cladded in my red dress and boots, I plucked up courage and drove out. It took me half an hour to reach there.

The place seemed hushed, as if everybody had gone home. Having cold feet, I walked slowly into the seminar room. Surprisingly, the organiser was still there waiting for me. She was indeed expecting me.

Upon greeting me, she enlightened me on how the talk had impacted many of the participants and most of them were keen to join the Beauty Pageant. She went through the entire talk with me again and encouraged me to join the competition.

Out of concern, I asked if this competition was meant for those who would like to improve their physical appearances from the worst to the best. That would mean it was more relevant for people with exterior beauty challenges as it was stated that every married woman is eligible to join. Just as Priscilla mentioned, she is already satisfied with all that she is. What more do we need to improve?

The organiser replied,

"Are you sure that you are that perfect and no improvements are needed?"

The question triggered me to think further. I thought to myself, was I really that satisfied and "perfect" to an extent I did not need further improvement.?

I thought to myself, was I really that satisfied and "perfect" to an extent I did not need further improvement?

Well, perhaps there was something that I could gain from being part in the Beauty Pageant?

May be there was something in there that I could benefit from. I could get some make-up tips, gain insights from the inner beauty training, or even learn how to catwalk, etc. In fact, I do not know how to make-up at all! Learning

make-up skills through the Beauty Pageant seems to be an ideal offer as professional make-up courses usually cost a fortune to sign-up. Besides, it has always been part of my value system that every woman should take part in a beauty pageant contest at least once in her life time in the quest of unleashing the "Perfect Woman" from within.

Participating in a beauty pageant contest is indeed a dream come true for many women. I had passed the prime season in my younger days to be part of a beauty pageant contest, never had I imagine I would be given the opportunity to fulfill my lifelong dream once again.

This Beauty Pageant Contest seems to be very different from the others. It was a nationwide contest with the provision of training.

The organiser assured me that every individual who went through the training would transform and became better. The end product will be an improved self.

"Come tomorrow to Butterworth for the first round of the Contest, Winnie. I look forward to seeing you. Bring along two photos of yours."

The organiser seemed to sound very confident that I would turn up the next day.

"Butterworth? That is quite a distance as I am living in Penang Island. How am I going to get there?"

I illustrated the entire story to my beloved hubby Max at home. Oblivious to what was about to be unravelled, Max sounded rather proud of me joining the Beauty Pageant, after which he regretted as you will discover in the latter part of this story.

"I can send you there." he offered.

Thank God! He didn't stop me from joining the Beauty Pageant. It was indeed encouraging seeing how much he supported my decision.

Shortly after, I received an SMS from the organiser.

"Winnie, if you are coming tomorrow, try not to dress up too stunningly. Just put yourself at a very low key for a start."

It seemed like the organiser was giving me a heads up. If I were to dress up too exquisitely for a start, it would not have portrayed any differences in the "before" and "after" effect of being transformed. After all, the theme of this competition was "From a Caterpillar to a Butterfly" which means turning from an ugly duckling into a swan.

That's the guideline. I would abide by the advice given.

THE CATERPILLAR

So the day came when the first round of contest begun. I was cladded in my jeans and a simple pink shirt. Quite modest and casual looking.

As I arrived, I noticed a few other ladies in their sexy attires seemingly experienced participants of the Beauty Pageant Contest. Insecurity crept in as the organiser advised me to maintain low profile for a start. How was I going to compete with these experienced pageants?

Nonetheless, observing the way these ladies communicate and dressed seemed to display a different impression, at least to me. Some of them did not appear to be that elegant after all. In fact, the way they carried themselves, coupled with their choice of clothes made them appear rather inappropriate and in spiteful description, downgraded in self-value.

"May be I am in the wrong place. I don't think I can fit in the circle of people I had just seen," I thought to myself.

Just as I was about to stand up to excuse myself, I saw one or two graceful ladies walked in. Feeling rather relieved, I reassured myself that there could have been a vast mixture of people from from different types of background joining this very competition.

I should not conclude from the first look of it and judge the book by its cover.

Even though we may come from different backgrounds and experiences in life, we still have something to learn from one another. Looking back from where I am now, I had to admit that it was not right for me to despise others as well. If our Father in Heaven is willing to mingle with people from all walks of life, who are we to deem others as unfitting to be associated with us?[1]

Soon after, the organiser began announcing for all the participants to take their seats. It was too late for me to leave.

"O.K. everyone. Thank you for your participation. Please fill in the application form and make a total payment of RM200 for our administration cost. Do remember to submit your photos as well. Apart from that, I would like for all of you to go home and write an essay on why you deserve to win this contest?"

Why do I deserve to win this contest? Yes, I had something in my mind to write. I intended to present all the money I won to my mum for her coming birthday in December as a birthday gift. By the time I completed the final round of Beauty Pageant contest, it would have been December and the timing was just perfect. My mum was overwhelmed when I told her my intended plan. If I were to win the competition, I would give her everything I won. Did I truly brought happiness to her with my decision of participating in this competition? As the story goes on, you will see how my decision had brought her worries and fears.

---

[1] Mark 2:15 While Jesus was having dinner at Levi's house, many tax collectors and sinners were eating with him and his disciples, for there were many who followed him.

"Alright. Ladies. Are you ready? Stand up from your seats. I need you to all to line up and step up the stage one by one. The judges will be interviewing you. All you need to do is answer the questions directed to you." the organiser instructed as she gathered the contestants.

Oh Gosh! Answering in Mandarin? That sounds like a big challenge for me. Although I was Chinese-educated in my schooling days, my Mandarin has become rusty with time. I mean I can speak a smattering of Mandarin but it was not exactly that fluent. I have forgotten the Chinese proverbs and beautiful phrases used in Mandarin literatures.

"O.K. I am going to show you how to perform a catwalk once through. After which, you will all catwalk on the stage. Follow closely how I walk. Stop at this point to answer to the questions given by the judges. Remember to be confident. Get it? Alright. Let's start from this lady here." the organiser continued directing.

So, the first lady went up and exuded confidence. I was truly impressed by the flowery phrases she employed in her answer. How was I going to present my answer then? And the catwalk! I have never done catwalk in my life. This is completely alien to me.

"It's alright," I thought to myself. Since the organiser did give me hints on being moderate for a start. I took it nonchalantly.

"Next. Next.... Next Winnie." the organiser announced.

And so my turn came. All I remembered was I walked very clumsily on the stage. And the audience burst into laughter.

The organiser then posed me a question.

"So tell me. Why did you come for the contest?"

As I was used to lecturing students, I did not answer with soft-spoken voice like some of the contestants. It would seem rather pretentious to me. I wanted to be myself, being true to who I really am.

On the spur of the moment, I answered the organiser bluntly. "My friend was reluctant to participate in this competition because she said this competition was for ugly and fat people and that she is already perfect and satisfied with who she is. But I thought I needed some personal improvement and I could learn make-up lessons for free here."

The audience burst into laughter again which I did not quite comprehend. It was not an intended humour but the audience took my clumsy catwalk as deliberate act of making myself a laughing stock.

After that day, I received another sms from the organiser congratulating me for passing the first round and that I could proceed to the next stage. So we were informed that the next event would be catwalk training session in the day and social etiquette, performance for the guests as well as dinner in the night. However, We were given home assignment and were required to hand in the home assignment on that very day i.e. evaluating our very own twenty strengths and twenty weaknesses in writing.

THE HOME ASSIGNMENT

I was burning the midnight oil trying to complete my assignment for the contest. The evaluation of my twenty strengths and twenty weaknesses had to be written in Mandarin. Recalling and refreshing my memory on certain Mandarin characters was a dread indeed. I was cracking my head finding twenty items. I could only think of ten. Realising that the coming Wednesday was another round of competition was truly enervating for me. This competition came out of the blue and it was really challenging for me to manage my schedule. I dared not dwell too much on it because it would stress me up.

As it was already late in the night, I went to bed. When I woke up, I discovered a few lines appended to the paper I scribbled last night: It was my hubby's handwriting contributing to the rest of the piece, as he was good in detecting the minor aspects of me.

1. Do not think before I speak...
2. Don't like to do housework...
3. Talk with a high pitch voice' like lecturing

.... and more.

Good. This would contribute to my list of twenty weaknesses. It saved up my time in completing the assignment given.

Mother suggested some weaknesses to me too. Of course one of them is 'stubborn' and 'does not listen to her'. It seemed like she had become very supportive of my decision to participate in the Beauty Pageant. When I told her about joining the competition initially, she was rather against it. Now it seemed as though she had changed her tune. She even taught me how to dress appropriately for the social etiquette evaluation test. Being very anxious to ensure I looked my best, she even picked out evening gowns from her wardrobe for me to try on. I almost turned her dressing room into a warzone sifting through everything in there. At last, I found something deemed for the night's occasion. I even had my handbag, watch and shawl on loan from her.

COMPETITION, CO-OPERATION

One of the contestants called me up to ask if I could give her a lift to the competition venue. I was trying to figure out how to help her to get to the next competition destination. Her home was rather far from where I was living. And I probably needed to meet her somewhere closer to my home in order to pick her up. We were discussing on how to make the most feasible arrangement.

On another occasion, I tried texting the organiser, asking her for tips on what to prepare for the competition the following day but she did not revert to me. Thankfully, I was generous enough to offer help to my friend when she needed a lift and she was not selfish to share whatever information she attained from another source. We were told to bring along a pair of jeans, high heels and to dress in casual attires in the afternoon.

The next day, this friend of mine called me up to inform me that there was no need for me to worry about her transportation because someone else who was staying nearby had offered to give her a lift.

What a great culture to cultivate in this competition i.e. Co-operation.

THE CATWALK

I had never come across catwalk in my life. I thought I'd better checked on You Tube to understand a little bit more about what this catwalk is all about. Who knows I may be able to pick up some basic skills from there and catch up a little bit faster during the training sessions.

I started blogging about joining Beauty Pageant Contest in my Facebook to retain my journey in joining the Beauty Pageant Contest. One of the things I like about Facebook is that our friends are able to keep track on how we are getting on with life from time to time. In any case something was not going well in life, Facebook followers are able to trace it from our blog posts.

If it was not Facebook, I would not be able to seek for help from a group of Christians community n my network who had been praying for me and supporting me in my quest of overcoming my ordeal.

To be honest, if it was not for Facebook, I would not have been able to seek help from a group of Christians community in my network who had been praying for me and supporting me in my quest of overcoming my ordeal.

I was becoming more serious about the competition. The next day, I made an appointment with France and Taipei Bridal studio to

have my make-up done for the next round of competition. I knew that this investment would help transform me into a star-looking face. Professional make-up does make a great deal of difference. Even ugly ducklings can have a chance to be turned into swans.

I arrived at the hall with my stiletto heels as we were requested to bring along our high heels for the catwalk training session. I got to know a few new friends that day. Some of them commented that I looked very much different from before. I then handed in my assignment and photos to one of the organisers.

The organiser hired a professional model to train us in catwalk. I did not recognise who she was as I was not familiar with the modelling world. All I knew was that this lady with an extremely svelte figure caught my attention from afar off. At first glance, she looked gorgeous and had a killer posture as she poised when she walked. Unlike most of the ladies, we sometimes do not have the habit of practising good posture, to the extend we even slouch. Now I knew that I had something to learn from this lady.

There was also another professional model involved in training us how to catwalk. We were asked to form a beeline up from the shortest to the tallest. It was then I realised there were a number of contestants who came from other states of the country. They had passed the preliminary round within their states and were sent to compete in the next round in Penanvg. The organiser is based in Penang. I was actually one of the two tallest ladies amongst the contestants.

We got our numbers and tied them around our wrists. The training was about to begin.

"Alright, ladies. I would like all of you to lean against the wall for at least fifteen minutes. with your head and back touching the wall.

The back of your head, your shoulder and your hip points must touch the wall. No talking. Make use of your time to work on your postures. We haven't had much time left." The trainer instructed.

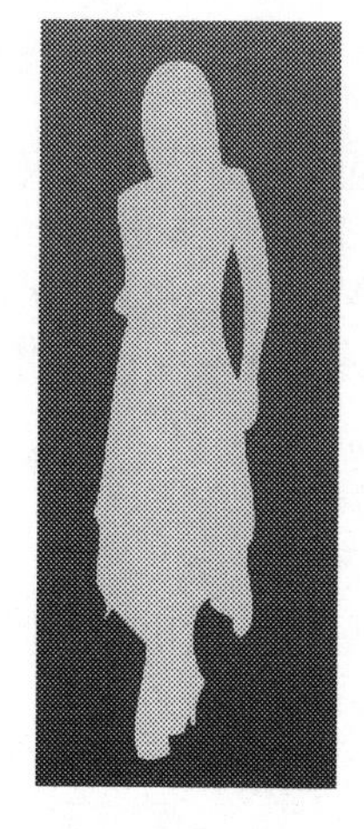

Approximately fifteen minutes had passed before the trainer said,

"Alright, ladies. How are you feeling? Tired? Now move away from the wall maintaining the same posture as you walk forward. This is the correct method for you to walk. Straight up and no slouching. If you feel as though your body is going back to its old habit, go back to the wall and lean against it again. Do this repeatedly for many times until your body get used to the correct posture." the trainer said.

"Now are you ready for the catwalk training? Now follow the way I walk closely. Relax your body and walk with an elegant style. Be bold and present yourself confidently. You must also pay very careful attention when you walk down the staircase. When you stumble and fall, it is going to be really embarrassing. Do not look down when you walk. Just get used to the steps on the stairs.

"Stand straight and keep your chest up at 180 degree. Maintain your posture and walk on the tip of your toes. When you are walking, your feet should land directly in front of the other foot instead of side by side. Put your arms by your side like this. When you reach the end of the stage, give the audience a cool swooned look. Turn your head slightly to the left and to the right. Stop at this point, strike a pose. Remember to walk to the other side. Strike a pose. And to the other side. Strike another pose. Walk to the next point here. Give a pose. Remember to walk in a triangular manner. Finally, catwalk back to the

centre. Stop, give the audience a smile and catwalk back to the back of the stage. This is all to be done for the solo catwalk." the trainer instructed as she demonstrated the catwalk for us.

The trainer continued to show us catwalk in pairs.

We were lining up like troops to practise our catwalk. The group was divided into two with one group being trained by the other trainer. Other veteran participants began to proactively involve in teaching others how to improvise their catwalks. The session was indeed a great deal of fun and I thoroughly enjoyed it.

"O.K. One by one. Relax. Off you go!"

"Music please." the trainer instructed.

Indeed, the music was totally upbeat and I was in the mood of performing a catwalk. It was my turn. Unknowingly, I had improved and I was arranged to perform my catwalk solo because of my height which is among the tallest.

Soon after, a young chap turned up during our training interrupting our practice as he asked us to change our catwalk choreography. He was the one in charge of leading the model line-up and instructed us on where we should go after each catwalk was performed.

They had a discussion on the numerous changes of points as to where we were supposed to stop and strike a pose during the catwalk.

We were also taught a different style of walking druing the training. After which, they made up their minds on the kind of catwalk we are supposed to perform before we were trained extensively toward it.

"Let's standardise it this way. It is easier for everyone."

"Music please." the trainer exclaimed.

All the models were lined up in a beeline. The contestants gave their best practicing the entire afternoon until we have all become experts in catwalk.

"Alright! Everyone. Some of you may take a break if you wish. Please be reminded that as you begin socialising during the break, that every action and demeanour of yours will be recorded. It will be taken into consideration as part of the competition's marking criteria." the organiser reiterated on and off to remind everybody to be conscious of their behaviour and that all eyes were on us evaluating our overall performances.

I had learnt a few valuable lessons on how to carry ourselves in social events. When we are in a socialising event, we should not stand there like wallflowers and become oblivious when we are in a social event. Sometimes it is understandable that we do not feel like entertaining anyone in certain occasions. Nonetheless, we should always keep in mind that no matter how anti-social we feel like at that moment, we must at least make an effort to talk to at least three people from the crowd. Once we are placed on the social platform, like it or not, we will be watched closely as a hawk eyeing on prey--how we dress, how we interact, how we socialise or even the way we eat or drink. All these will no longer be subjected to privacy as soon as we live under the limelight.

THE STARRING NIGHT

This was the moment when everybody had been waiting for. The guests were about to arrive.

"Alright, Angels-to-be. Are you ready for the show tonight? Quickly change into your beautiful dresses."

All the contestants started dressing up in their evening gowns. The changing room was a warzone. Everyone was preoccupied with getting their hair and make-up done. I had my make-up and hair-do done earlier on at France and Taipei bridal studio. So there was nothing much for me to work on except changing into my black evening gown. Draping my mum's furry shawl around my shoulders and clutching the handbag with the string around my wrist, I was all ready for the starring night.

With that long, sleek evening gown, it was actually very easy for me to hide my weaknesses while performing the catwalk as no one could actually see my legs when I walked. For those who wore pants or short skirts, their challenge would be to perform a perfect catwalk.

A few people started to suspect that I was involved in the modelling. In actual fact I was in a different industry altogether. Someone even commented that I looked like one of the Hong Kong superstars and

I thought France and Taipei Bridal Studio professional make-up and hairdo made a very good job in con- tribution to that.

After preparing, we went for an early dinner in the restaurant. On each of the reserved dining table, there was a sign written 'Mrs. Malaysia'. I was beyond astonishment, thinking to myself, "This could not be the Mrs. Malaysia World Pageant pre-selection." The competition language was in Chinese and Mrs. Malaysia Beauty Pageant Competition has always been in English.

Perhaps this was true as I read from a blog that in the past Mrs. Malaysia World 2008 was launched to select a Malaysian representative to compete in Mrs. World 2009 held in Vung Tau, Vietnam on

22 November, 2009. However, due to sponsorship matters, the pageant was never held on the proposed date.

With pride and joy, I called Max and informed him that the contest might lead to winning the 'Mrs. Malaysia' title to represent the country to compete internationally. I tried finding out more from the other contestants who were sitting in the same table. I came to realise that many of them were from different states all over Malaysia such as Ipoh, Johor, K.L., Penang, Butterworth, and so forth. It was a nationwide competition for the title 'Angel God' indeed. But why did they put down 'Mrs. Malaysia'? I tried finding out more by asking the waitresses around the room. One of them mentioned that her superior did not know what Beauty Pageant Contest was going on exactly. Hence, he simply adopted the name 'Mrs. Malaysia'.

"O.K. Ready. Angels-to-be. Have you finished your dinner? The guests were here. Get ready. Find your groups and line up.

There are two entrance points. I want each of you to pose with your arms at the side, give the audience a big smile when you step out onto the stage. The judges are right below. So mind the stairs when you walk down."

The reporters arrived soon after. They interviewed the organiser and waited for the performance to start.

"Music on!"

I could hear a flurry of excitement amongst the audiences. I was peeping from the backstage. Some of the contestants had started performing. One by one, they walked down posing and performing their catwalk.

"Get ready! Get ready!" The leader was quite stern in ensuring that we stay in our lines and groups.

Two more contestants in front and it would be my turn. I was very anxious to perform next.

Then my turn came. It is quite challenging to walk with long skirt and high heels on the stairs as if you accidentally step on your dress, you may trip and fall. I had to lift up my dress slightly while I walked. But I managed with my other hand holding my hanging bag on my wrist. I was arranged to walk solo. As contestants walked out, their names would be announced with their ages and the number of children they have had. This helped the judges to remember the contestants.

Strutting towards the stopping points with long strides, I posed a cool look at the audience whilst turning my head left and right. Then at the very end I gave the audience a charming smile.

The night truely made me feel like a star as I enjoyed the camera shots and video shoot aiming at me. It was indeed a dream come true for me as I always wonder how it felt like being part of a beauty pageant contest. Whenever I saw the beauty pageant competitions on television, I would envy wistfully and thought if only I was young again. After getting married, most women will have past the prime time for that. Thank God, I had the chance to be part of this experience again. Well, at least for that moment, I felt that way.

It was indeed a dream come true for me as I always wonder how it felt like being part of a beauty pageant contest.

Notwithstanding the immense pain that I had to bear in the middle of my Metamorphosis--now looking back--I think the ending part was rewarding. Without further ado, I would end the anticipation of all

readers, welcoming you to a chapter that allows readers to experience the climax, grief, anxiety, curiosity from what came next in this story.

We were asked to perform a few rounds before the announcement of the results were made. I was short-listed with approximately more than twenty other candidates out of the total of sixty contestants that took part in the semi-final round.

The reporters took group photographs of us and we were allocated to different groups according to the states we originate from. Each group has a leader.

"O.K. Angels-to-be. Are you excited about what is coming up next? The next session is a compulsory training session for everyone. It will last for ten hours, five hours for the first day and five hour for the second day. You must complete the training. Otherwise, your participation will be forfeited. Wear loose, casual clothing. T-shirts and pants are fine."

At this stage, everything seemed to be transparent and normal for a typical Beauty Pageant Contest. What I was about to experience come was the ten-hour spiritual renewal session that I failed to get through.

8

THE SPIRITUAL TRAINING

As usual, Max showed his support for me by driving me to the training venue. I was still basking in the afterglow of last night's performance and looked forward to the next challenge.

"Wear loose clothing" was the instruction given to us--I abided in the given instructions. I was dressed in my casual T-shirts and pants. However, I did not feel comfortable as I wore my slimming lingeria on the inside. It was really tight.

As soon as I set foot into the centre, I could feel the spiritual atmosphere. It gave me an impression that this was kind of a religious place. It is not a Buddhist centre. Neither is it a Christian centre. I could not comprehend which religion it is but I knew it is originated from Taiwan.

As the training started, he asked each of us to make a vow--a promise to keep this training a secret from others for fear that untoward things may happen to us. He gave us a testimony of what this religion did to him when he broke his vow. The trainer confessed that when he was younger, he had a roving eye for pretty girls and a strong urge to rape them. He could not control himself. I could not recall whether he confessed he actually raped girls before or not, but he felt guilty of his lecherous behaviour.

He repented and in his religion if one had lustful intention toward a girl, his eyes would become swollen and painful the very next day. He was fond of the consequences that result of his action, which was derived as a punishment. This would keep him disciplined. He also shared his fear of darkness ever since he was young. He was so fearful that he had to sleep with the lights on. Every time the light was switched off, he would feel really insecure. As he grew up, he felt a prompting in his heart to work with spirits and he felt he was given a mission in this world.

"Now I am going to bring all of you back to your past life and if you feel guilty about anything in your heart, please frell free to express it. Help yourself with the tissue papers here if you can't resist and cry out."

I was flabbergasted and frightened by the surrounding of people wailing.

The trainer then asked everyone to close their eyes and lights in the room were being switched off. Feeling paranoid and uncomfortable with what they were doing, I did not fully shut my eyes.

"What do you see, people?" asked the trainer.

All of a sudden, a few of the contestants began whimpering and they pouring out a lot of personal guilt they were feeling from within. I was flabbergasted and being frightened by the surrounding of people who were wailing in the room. Some of them even went to the extent of summoning back lost souls and asked for forgiveness from their deceased loved ones.

"Winnie, you are not concentrating. Close your eyes. What do you see?" the trainer spoke as he realised my attention was divided. I forced myself to close my eyes willy-nilly. His question prompted me

to go further and I saw an increasing luminescence of white light in the darkness.

"What do you see actually? Tell me."

I tried visualising and I saw myself lost and floundering in the jungle. My head and eyeballs began to look upward. I felt frightened, worried and insecure. Everybody pinpointed that I was struggling with a problem from within as I was fidgeting in my seat.

"Winnie, what is wrong with you? You seem to have a lot of problems. Pour out to us." the trainer prompted further.

"Nope, I am fine. I don't have any problems. I have been very happy all these while. Problems are created by our own doing. If we keep on thinking we have problems, problems will come." I responded.

"Winnie, you are not honest with us. Be involved." the trainer said.

To be truthful, I did not have any problems. My problem stemmed from this workshop. The reason why I seemed to have so many struggles was because I was frightened by the stories told by the candidates. After crying and weeping, all of them were refreshed and renewed.

Now the only person left unrenewed was me. I was very disturbed by the activities in the hypnosis session. I was quite a happy woman before involving in this beauty pageant contest. Why do I now feel as though I had a lot of unsolved problems I dared not face it?

I was quite a happy woman before involving in this beauty pageant contest. Why do I now feel as though I had a lot of unsolved problems I dared not face it?

The training ended for the day. There was another similar five-hour training the next day. While waiting for Max to pick me up, I bumped into the trainer outside the training centre. He had a word with me. He told me that I would definitely be back the next day. I was planning on giving up as I dreaded the thought of going back to join them again. But that night I could hardly sleep a wink--I felt the sense of incompleteness within me. Perhaps I should go back to complete the ten hour training. Then I would be healed.

The next day, I went early. In fact, I was the first person to arrive at the training centre. This time, I followed the instructions given by the trainer closely. Loose and comfortable outfit it was. I had a brief chat with the trainer before the session started. He recommended me some books from Taiwan while waiting for the others to come.

As soon as the rest arrived, the trainer began his training session. "Now Angels God-to-be, I am going to bring you for a tour up heaven today. Assuming that it is 2012 The End Times, we are about to watch what happen to each one of you. Close your eyes now and I will switch off the light soon. Winnie, you must participate this time, alright?" the trainer insisted.

"Alright." I answered reassuringly.

The trainer began his hynosis process on all of us by asking questions.

"What do you see? What do you see?Angels God-to-be?" he asked.

Each of us went in a trance and one of the contestants started getting excited, "I see white light and flowers. Many trees…." she exclaimed.

"What else?"

"I see something spinning in front. It looks like the lotus."

"Same here. I see the same thing." uttered the other contestant.

"I see a small flower lying there very lonely." I spoke correspondingly.

"Winnie, seems like your visualisation is vivid today. Why is the flower very lonely?" the trainer asked.

"Because no one cares for it."

"O.K. Talk to the flower. Water it. Now, what do you see?"

"I see it growing bigger and bigger. And it blooms to become really really beautiful."

"So, the lesson learnt here is that we must learn to love and care for the objects placed around us. Talk to these objects. They all have spirits. Even the non-living things have spirits. If you want to sell your products well, just learn to communicate with your products, instructing them to attract your customers everyday. They will work miracles for you. This is the basic teaching in our religion." the trainer explained.

"Good idea. Why not we use it for our company's products to get more customers?"

I overheard a few of them from the same company exchanging conversation. I was sceptical about the advice. Being judgmental, I felt this was an unethical way of enticing the customers into buying

products. If the products meet a high standard in quality, I am sure the products can be sold even without the application of this technique.

Despite the contrary, I suppose people do employ different strategies in making their products sell such as consulting Feng Shui Master, Talisman, Amulets, and so forth.

"Angel Gods-to-be, there is another lesson I have prepared for you. Which of you have children of your own? Do you know why your children fall sick sometimes? It's because they need love and attention from you." the trainer explained as he moved on to the following lesson.

"O.K. Angels God-to-be. Go further. What do you see? Come on, people. Tell me."

"O.K. Angels God-to-be. I would like for you to go deeper into your visualisation. Now, what do you see? Come on, people. Tell me." prompted the trainer.

"I see a figure who looks like Goddess of Mercy sitting on the lotus." one of the contestants exclaimed.

"I see the same thing too." another snapped. "Well done people. We are all at the same place." The trainer guided us into a deeper trance.

"I see Jesus's face looking down towards the earth. He looks really sad. He kept shaking his head. Oh no. He is crying."

"I feel the cooling sensation. It's so comfortable. Where am I now?"

"Winnie. You are up here." the trainer reassured me.

"Heaven? It feels so comfortable here. Oh! I don't feel like leaving this place."

I was in a state of euphoria--moving into the realm of fantasy of the so-called heaven.

"I can take you here anytime. I have been travelling around the universe quite often." said the trainer.

"Have some water, Winnie."

The trainer passed me a pack of mineral water to me with a straw readily placed in it. I took a few sips and relaxed. I was so tired these few days that I dozed off unconsciously during the training. In semi-conscious state, I heard some commotion going on. Some of the participants were unable to enter into this so-called heaven to join the rest. Others were trying to reach out to those who were seen screaming for help. I overheard their attempt in giving solutions to those who are unable to enter "heaven" by urging each of them to repent of her sins.

I was so tired these few days that I dozed off and unconsciously during the training.

"So who will be the next Angel God? Why are all of you here? Why do you think you deserve to be crowned the next Angel God?" The trainer asked at the top of his voice. We were pelted by questions after questions by the trainer. The trainer sounded as though he was interviewing each and everyone of us.

"I have what it takes to be an Angel God because I want to save mother earth!" someone asserted spontaneously with great tenacity. It

sounded as though she was prompted by the holy spirit from within to answer these questions. Her voice reverberated differently.

"I have given up so much on my family for this competition. I deserve to win. My hubby had been calling me so often to complain how much I have neglected the family because of this competition. I must win!" another person exclaimed firmly.

"We have come all the way from Johor. We paid for our own hotels and travelling expenses. Not to mention about the expensive clothes that we have invested for the competition. That's how much we have sacrificed for this competition and we really hope that we can get somewhere."

"Winnie?" the trainer insisted.

"Well, it is up to the organisers to decide. If I win the title, I will give the prize money to my mum because her birthday is just around the corner. To me, she is an Angel God." I replied.

"Winnie, if you win, you must take the credit and accept the prizes yourself. You should not honour anyone. Your mother is not the Angel God." the trainer insisted.

Within me, I had fear of winning the title. It made me cringe for I did not know what their mission was for the champion of this competition. Surely the organiser would not throw out a big sum of money just to search for an Angel God. There must be something that they wanted the Angel God to do. Perhaps being an ambassador for the products they are selling, I don't know.

But since the selection involved spiritualism, I was more sceptical about their mission. One thing for sure, I did not want to convert my original religion.

"By the way, everyone. If you feel insecure about another person being more competent than you, give that person a hug and miracles will happen. Remember what I said to you," instructed the trainer.

"All right. Angels God-to-be, we are going down to the earth now."

I felt the heat around me, the heavenly feeling surrounded me slowly subsided.

"Where are we now?" I asked. "We are going back to the earth."

"So fast? I want to stay in heaven for a little longer. It's just so comfortable. Can we go back and let me experience it again?"

The trainer laughed.

"Alright. Let's go back to 'heaven'. I can bring you there anytime." claimed the trainer.

"So what do you think of the heavenly feeling? Wasn't it great? Do you think you would still want to go back to the earth to suffer after this experience? Will you miss your family?"

"It feels great! We want to linger here a little longer." the contestants responded.

"Winnie, I see you are sitting next to Jesus. Will anyone in this room win? Will anyone in this room win?" The trainer seemed to be consulting his guide.

"Time to go back now, everyone. We can have our meeting in 'heaven' the next time." joked the trainer.

I felt the heat surrounding me. I saw the traffic and people being caught up with the hustle and bustle of life below me. I could not comprehend why it seemed as though everyone was in a hurry. I started descending further and further down. Time seemed to be really slow up in 'heaven'.

"Now you may slowly open your eyes. You have now arrived back on earth." the trainer declared.

Reluctantly, I opened my eyes and looked at my watch. To my astonishment, it was already approximately three in the afternoon. I felt as if the hynosis experience had only lasted for what seemed like a short while.

One of the contestants stood up from amidst and came to offer me a hug. I was puzzled and did not understand why. Perhaps it was done out of joy as we had all landed on earth safely. I accepted her offer and we hugged each other.

"Let's go out for lunch together. Like I said, we can always call for a meeting in 'heaven'. But, remember, you must keep the event that had happened to day a secret. Or else untoward things will happen to you. Or even if you speak out, others may deem you as being out of your mind. So keep this training a secret." emphasised the trainer.

"Excitement, fear, anxiety, separation, and death are part of the process of a caterpillar turning into a butterfly."

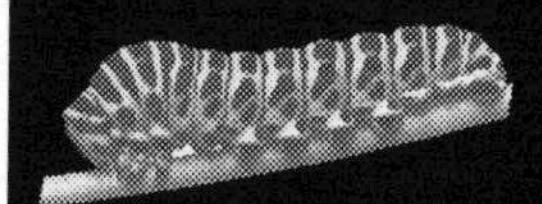

We proceeded to have our lunch together that evening. During lunch time, I had this feeling that the trainer was trying to avoid eye contact with me while conversing. His demeanour appeared to be enigmatic. It looked to me that he had guilt from within as his voice was stifled as he spoke. Nonetheless, I had fun chatting with the other ladies on everything and anything under the sun. Indeed, I felt much more relaxed and relieved compared to the day before.

I had no intention to go against the organiser by publishing this book. This is merely a simple sharing of my personal experiences. Should the organiser decides to confront or take action against all that I have uttered with regards to this competition, I am ready to face them in the presence of my Lord.

If only I had the chance to go through the video playback of this part of my life, I would like to watch it all over again. I could not fathom why I was obsessed with it. Indeed, it seemed as though I was wondering in the wilderness for forty days (approximately 6 weeks from the end of October to early December). However, I strongly believed that things do happen for a reason. I have to thank the organiser for organising this event. If I had not joined this contest, I would not have been come to Christ.

THE TRANSFORMATION PROCESS

Call it transformation process of a caterpillar or ordeal or what. When I came home that night, I just did not feel like going back to the competition again. I recoiled at the thought of untoward incident which seemed imminent. I felt that my entire house was creepy. Literally, I was afraid to set foot into every corner of my house--the toilets, the bedrooms, the living room, etc. I had not been sleeping well for many nights because every night my mind was immersely disturbed.

Literally, I did not dare to step into my toilet, my room and every corner of my house.

That night, I felt as though my whole body was being controlled. My hand was lifted up involuntarily in the middle of the night. At that instant, I felt as though being strangled. The suffocation made me feel better off dying being in Heaven as compared to this place.

Early next morning, I rushed off to the Tzu Chi organisation. I still remember bringing a handy recorder with me playing the Buddhist song record in hope for protection from any harmful spirits. Nonetheless, the player somehow dropped hard on the floor and was completely broken. So much so that the cassette inside was damaged as well.

I was in a dishevelled state. I could not imagine myself wearing my black robe (Hai Qing)just to reassure myself that I was protected while driving. Passer-by who saw me would have thought that I had gone insane.

I arrived at the Tzu Chi organisation safe and sound at approximately six in the morning. I quickly took part in the chanting session and burst into tears in front of a sister there. She did not know what was wrong with me. I remembered vividly we sat on the staircase outside in the open air after the chanting session. I was at a loss for words and she was trying to piece together what I was trying to articulate.

I stammered as he first sentence came out from my mouth, "Sister, I.. I--" I stuttered.

'.. encountered with a spiritual attack." I could not continue as I wept helplessly.

I felt as though I was being gagged and did not dare to elaborate much. She could not understand me at all.

"Sister, in order for me to help you, you need to tell me the whole story." the sister insisted.

I shook my head indicating that I was having trouble and it was inconvenient to share.

I uttered the phrase, "Beauty Pageant Contest."

She still did not quite get it. But she could more or less interprete what I was trying to express.

"Sister, when your heart is calm, no evil spirit will come near you. Trust me." she spoke meekly.

"I do not want to go home. My home is not safe. I don't want to leave here. Please allow me to stay on here." I pleaded.

"Sister, remember what I've said. When your heart is calm, evil spirit cannot fluster you. Compose yourself! Just stay calm and don't focus on it. Carry on your daily activities. The more you think about it, the more you are inviting the spirit to come near you."

The sister reiterated the word 'Stay calm' a few times and advised me to go home.

"Try it. And tomorrow if you still encounter the same problem, look for me. I am here to help you." the sister assured me.

Indeed, the problem did not stop. Not even when I tried staying calm and forcefully stopped myself from thinking about the situation. The eerie sensation did not fail to haunt me wherever I set foot into my house- There was no peace. I felt as if I was in a living hell. I did not even have the courage to use my very own master bed room toilet. I was so fearful to take my shower in my children's bathroom. I even moved all my toiletries to their bathroom.

I broke into cold sweat during night time. When night fell, I felt as though I was under attack by countless spirits. The strangling, the pulling, the needle prickling feeling were felt all over my body. Max was sleeping soundly besides me and I was totally envious of him. I just could not bring myself to close my eyes. As a matter of fact, I even switched on the balcony light for a better sense of security.

Everyday at the crack of dawn, as soon as I saw my maid, I followed her everywhere she went. From the kitchen to the dining room. From the dining room to the back and to the front.

I was paranoid. I just needed someone to be around me. And wherever I went, I would have the lights switched on everywhere--it made me feel safe.

I did not turn up for the subsequent rounds although I was short-listed. They invited me via text messaging again and again. In fact, they did not mind that I was absent for once. But truth be told, I could not be bothered with what programme came next. All I wanted was to get back to my normal life.

I just needed someone to accompany me. And wherever I went in the house, I would switch on the light very brightly just to feel secure.

I decided to return to Tzu Chi organisation. I felt that I really needed God the most during that time. As soon as I arrived at the hall, I saw Master Cheng Yen's photo hung on the wall, I bowed down and prayed. She is still alive. Although I knew that she is not the God, I had no God to turn to and had no other choice but to bow down and worshipped her picture. I was desperate.

The sister saw me, came by and asked me how I got on the night before. I started crying. I felt compelled to keep my experiences in the Beauty Pageant Contest a secret as I felt that I was under supervision. This time, more sisters were there to comfort me. At that point, they were busy doing some charity work in the organisation. I volunteered to help out and was very reluctant to return home. All I wanted to do was to stay there feeling protected.

“If you feel safer staying here, you may stay back and watch Da Ai T.V. channel. You can also help us with some glue work over here.” one of the sisters reassured me. I accepted their offer. Not long after, my mum dropped by Tzu Chi and asked to see me. She was worried sick.

“What are you doing here? Come home with me. Go back.” my mum firmly insisted.

“Mum, leave me alone. I am old enough to take care of myself.” I protested.

“What’s wrong with you? Do you want to see a doctor?”

“No. Mum. You don’t understand. Just leave me alone, please. I will be home soon.”

“Sister, we will take care of your daughter. Don’t worry. She will go home later.” one of the sisters in Tzu Chi organisation assured my mum.

“Are you sure you can take care of yourself?” mum asked in a worried tone.

“Yes, don’t worry. I will be alright.”

“Call me if you need help. Don’t linger here too long. Go home earlier. O.K.?” my mum implored.

The sister at Tzu Chi organisation exchanged a few words with my mum before she left.

“Sister, why not I bring you to meet a monk later? He is good at casting out evil spirits. Before that I will take you to the Ang Hock Si

Buddhist Temple. You can pray there and I will also bring you to meet someone there." the sister suggested.

"O.K." I agreed almost immediately.

I was brought to see a monk there. They did some rituals, splashed holy water on my head and invited me to go back to the temple to chant everyday if I could.

Thereafter, I went to another Siamise temple where the splashing of holy water was also performed on me.

"Do you want more protection? I can bring you to another monk." the sister offered.

The sister from Tzu Chi drove me to another temple to look for yet another monk.

"You don't look right. Sister." the monk claimed.

All I knew was I was constantly in semi-conscious state. My head and eyeballs often rolled upward and my head was spinning as if the spirit within me was fearful of the monk. The oppression was indeed strong.

"Don't tell me any story of yours. Everyone comes to me with a story to tell. Now the problem comes psychologically. You just need to ignore it. Keep yourself busy and it will vanish one day. Now I will chant for the spirit to leave you. Then you will be fine."

I heard the murmuring chants surrounding me. All of a sudden, he hollered the last powerful word at the very end of the ritual and

I felt as though I was awaken up from semi-consciousness state. "Is that it?" I asked.

It did feel like I was completely cured. I was over the moon and it felt as though everything was back to its normal state.

I was so grateful to the monk and the sister at Tzu Chi organisation that I offered to donate to the temple as a token of gratitude before I went home.

However, things changed when I returned home. As soon as I stepped into the house, the oppression began. Oh Gosh! How long will this torture last?

For the next few days, I visited many other temples to have holy water being splashed on me. I consistently joined a number of chanting sessions.

I even brought a few tape recorders with Buddhist's songs in them. I recalled an event whereby I brought my tape recorder along with me to my tuition class because I felt compelled to listen to Buddhist songs whenever I was driving, walking and even when I was in my classes, I did not seize listening to these songs with a headphone.

I remember taking a tape recorder with me to my tuition class. I had to listen to Buddhist songs when driving, walking and even in class with a headphone.

I had cancelled my classes a few times during the course of the Beauty Pageant contest. And when I stepped into my class to resume lessons, one of my students who arrived early

I had cancelled my classes a few times during the course of the Beauty Pageant contest. And when I stepped into my class to resume lessons, one of my students who arrived early asked me,

"So how was the competition, teacher? I heard news that you are short-listed in the Beauty contest."

My adult student seemed to be very proud of my achievement in the contest.

I did not know how to respond to the statement. I still had my tape recorder inside my handbag and I was still listening to the Buddhist song over and over again through the headphone. I just gave him a cryptic smile. I couldn't share anything. There was so much restriction. I was under Satan's supervision. I had this gripping fear that if I had spoken a single word about the event, I would be under attack during the night.

Throughout that period, I had many different kinds of spiritual encounters. Once when I was sleeping on one side on my bed, I felt a pressure pressing against my spine blocking me from turning to the other side. Then I was prevented from screaming. I had to struggle for a very long time before breaking free. Sometimes when my eyes were closed, I would see a spider. All these were not life threatening. The ones which truly made me feel sick were experiences of needle pricking on my body, throttling and tongue pulling torture.

I could not fall back asleep each time I was awaken by the torture.

Sometimes the torture was so unbearable that I wondered what I had done wrong in my life that I deserved to go through living like hell on earth.

Feeling helpless, I began surfing the internet in the wee hours. Most of my time was spent logging on to Facebook. Once when I was surfing the internet in the middle of the night, there came an ominous silence in the atmosphere. It was approximately 2 a.m. in the morning. The surrounding was so quiet that one could literally hear a pin drop. Out of a sudden, I heard a thud. A bunch of keys which were hung on the wall dropped onto the floor. It was truly spine-chilling. Many could have deemed it as a conincidence. Probably the keys were not hung properly on the wall, but it caused me to wonder why that bunch of keys only drop onto the floor at that particular hour?

Sometimes the torture was so unbearable that I wondered what I had done wrong in my life that I deserved to go through living like hell on earth.

I was outrageously fazed and could not hold it together any longer. I might be driven into mental disorder had I not found the solution to getting out of the spiritual malaise.

10

A CRY FOR HELP IN FACEBOOK

I had no where to appeal for help because in real life, people around me did not understand what had happened to me. I was often questioned,

"What's wrong with you? If you don't tell us the full story, how then are we able to help you?"

I tried revealing my story bit by bit--it was never completely uttered. Each time I tried revealing something, I would experience spiritual attacks in the midnight.

No one around me in reality could grasp what I was trying to express. Therefore, I had no choice, but to turn to Facebook. I thought of several ways to leave hints for others to pick up through Facebook that I was in deep trouble. I even tried umpteenth times on rephrasing my sentences. However, I never successfully hit the "Send" button because something kept holding me back. I even deleted a lot of direct appeals for help.

At this juncture, I tried tracing back my Facebook walls in 2009 and I wrote something on the wall that goes like this when a friend of mine asked me what was wrong with me.

"I don't know. I just happen to come across this competition in the press by chance. It is called 'Experiencing a caterpillar becoming a butterfly'. It is a search for Angel cum 'Mrs. Malaysia' by going through a series of courses. I wasn't aware that there were spiritual things involved. I just want to get back to my normal happy life."
November 6, 2009 at 6:26am • Like

I knew that I could have violated Facebook rules by sharing something inappropriate. I recalled going to a doctor asking for sleeping pills because I was suffering from insomnia. I shared with her about my reviewing my health condition in Facebook. She rebuked me by saying,

"We are not suppose to tell people about our health condition or reveal something really personal in Facebook. Facebook's purpose is for socialising."

To me, I had no choice. I felt I needed help badly. My incessant postings were becoming annoying to a handful of people and it caught a lot of attention from many others.

One of the most disturbing postings I've ever posted on my Facebook wall was as below:-

"...I felt heavy today and fear that I might sleep forever..."

At that point, I remembered there was an acquaintance who became really annoyed by my posts and removed me from his network. I even had friends who wrote to me on my Facebook wall suggesting that I should consider buying insurance for myself. There were a few friends who sensed something was amiss and they began tracing my posts from the past. Some wrote me personal messages. Others

called me from afar to check if I was alright. I was connected to some acquaintances who have become very good friends, and we maintained that closeness even after the ordeal. Amongst all, Benjamin was the messenger of Christ who offered me to receive the salvation of Jesus in one of my last days struggling with all these spiritual attacks.

There were Christians who referred me to different pastors out of goodwill to see if these pastors would be able to help me through my issues.

MARTA'S MEMORY

I remember madam used to be a cheerful person before she entered the Beauty Pageant Contest. As long as I have worked with her, I had never seen her going through depression before.

Madam spent most time with me in the house. I remember ever since she came back from the Beauty Pageant Contest, she lost her appetite; at times she did not even eat at all for two full days. I cooked oat and porridge for her. Sir was extremely concerned about her condition and often secretly checked with me to find out if madam had had her food. Her mother was also worried sick as she always followed up with me to see if there were improvements in her wellbeing several times in a day.

As long as I have worked for her, I had never seen her going into depression before.

I also remembered she was so fearful of using the washroom, to an extent she made me wait for her outside the washroom each time she had to use it. She often used her son's washroom and not her own masterbedroom's washroom.

I was worried about her and sometimes I prayed for her in Jesus name as I am a Christian. I even called back and asked my family member back in Indonesia to look for a Christian pastor who was well-known in the gift of healing to keep her in prayer.

Testimony paraphrased from an interview with my housekeeper, Marta Sallu who has worked under my household for six years. In fact, it was Marta who had reminded me about times when I lost my appetite as I had completely forgotten about it.

THE NEAR DEATH EXPERIENCE

I was getting weaker and weaker by night as I fought against the countless attacks. It seemed as though death was imminent. The torture made me feel I was better off dead. I had no fear of dying because heaven is a better place. I still missed that moment of experience I had in the so-called heaven during the spiritual training session when I was taking part in the Beauty Pageant. Besides, having had to bear with the suffocation of being strangled every single night made me feel as though I was already residing in hell.

I started to contract a really bad cough very badly everyday and felt nauseous. My health condition was deteriorating and becoming more and more worrying that I needed to go to Gleneagles Medical Centre to see a General Practitioner.

There was once I had a false alarm that I would be hospitalised the next day. So, I was busy packing in the middle of the night, preparing to be admitted into the hospital. However, nothing happened the next morning.

In another occasion, I went for a reflexology treatment and massage to relax myself. To my surprise, my legs and my whole body were feeling numb. I did not experience any pain at all which was strange as reflexology would normally inflict a certain amount of pain.

Now it seems as though my body's senses were eventually dying. Sometimes I felt nauseous but I was not able to purge at all.

Eventually, I was physically and mentally exhausted. I was too enervated to even walk and my spirit was almost totally drained out. I was actually about to have my birthday party in a couple of days. Instead of feeling all excited and hopeful, I was visualising that very day of my birthday as the day of my funeral.

Instead of feeling all excited and hopeful, I was visualising that very day of my birthday as the day of my funeral.

I donned my black robe and played the Buddhism music cassette to sleep every night, just in case I left this world and could no longer wake up the next morning.

If I woke up still alive the very next day, I would look very pale as though I was dying.

Literally, I even held the hands of my children tightly and spent time with them one of the nights thinking that that was the last night I spent with them.

I remembered that very night I asked Max a question,

"Darling, tell me that you love me. Then I will not leaving this world."

He thought I was totally out of my mind to have a morbid interest in death. He was truly frustrated with the whole matter. The Beauty Pageant Contest and the aftermath had taken a toll on him. I could tell that he regretted letting me participate in the Beauty Pageant. Nonetheless, it was too late.

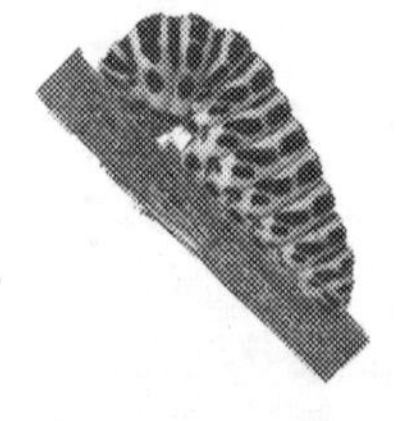

He did not tell me he loved me. I was totally heartbroken. He scooted towards the toilet and turned on the tap as he said to me,

"I think you are too tired. You need to relax. Take a hot shower. And dip your legs into the pail. This is the therapeutic for you. Just do as I say." he commanded.

I was forced to have a shower and was soaking wet from top to toe. I felt as if I wanted to give up living. He did not understand what was going on in my world. I really needed an affirming hug and comfort from him. But he was lack of sensitivity to understand me.

There was nothing in this world that seems worthwhile to keep me alive. I thought to myself, "Time for me to leave." Since no one was able to understand the torturous ordeal I was going through every night by things that were unseen, I was better off leaving this world. I began to imagine that if I was ever found dead, may be it would have been labelled the 'Mysterious Sickness' or 'Sudden Death'.

The room light was switched off and Max started to fall asleep slumbering like a baby.

The suffocation began. After sometime feeling as though I was being strangled and smothered to death, I began to choke and started coughing terribly. Eventually, I felt my tongue being pulled out by an invisible force. I struggled for a while.

However, after going through the torment for a while, there was a gap of peaceful hours in the midnight. This allowed me to write down my will during the period of peaceful moments. So I took out two pieces of paper to pen down my will and chance to remind Max to choose my favourite photo whereby I was dressed in red for my

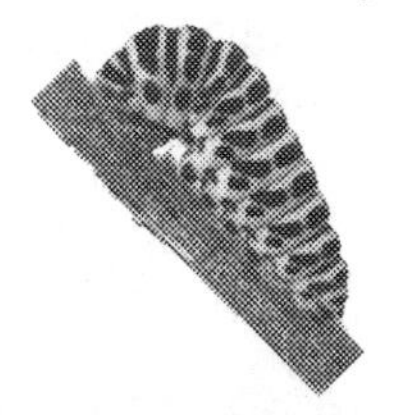

funeral. I remembered drafting out plans for my mum to take care of my kids when I am gone and gave all the money in my purse to my maid. I wrote down instructions on how to obtain the locker keys and everything else which I deemed to be important. I even reminded Max not to forget to dress me up in my black robe and put the two passports (which would enable me an easier entry to heaven) together with me in my casket when I leave the world.

Photo of red dress for the funeral

I even sent a student of mine a text message to bid farewell in the midnight. I suddenly dawned upon me that I had no time to search for a candidate to takeover my business. I felt like my spirit was about to leave my body. So I quickly screened through my contacts and found this person by the name of Benjamin.

It was quite peculiar of me to appeal help from an acquaintance like Benjamin. He was only my one-time customer. Little did he know what was revolving my life during that period. However, he had sent me text messages several times before this to ask how I was because I posted worrying status on my Facebook wall. I was touched by his willingness to offer help even though it was in the wee hours of the morning sometimes.

I was not given an opportunity to plan ahead. I felt my strength ebbing away and I would be dying very soon. Immediately I sent a text to Benjamin.

sent on the 9-11-09, time 1.41am

If anything happens 2 me and u r interested in marketing de books + b.games, call xxxxxxxx for my mother. I hope the real God will b by my side. Tq.

I remembered receiving an immediate reply offering to lead me to Christ. I was already in a perplexed state. I could not understand what Benjamin was trying to attempt in confusing me even further as it was rather disturbing for me to hear of another God in my final hour. I was all prepared to follow Buddhism when coming face to face with death.

I replied courteously, informing Benjamin that I was already a Buddhist and intended to remain that way. He wrote back convincing me to put my trust in Jesus' hand and have faith in Him. I did not have much choice then as I felt I was at the brink of death.

I was actually prepared to be tormented to death. All I was hoping was for a GOD (any God) to come, greet me and take me to HEAVEN to end my suffering.

"Why does Jesus come into the picture now? My mind was a one-track mind i.e. to follow Buddha for the rest of my life. It's so confusing," I thought to myself. Nonetheless, these questions caused me to begin opening up my mind to seek the true and living GOD. Who is my true GOD? The two names popped up in my mind

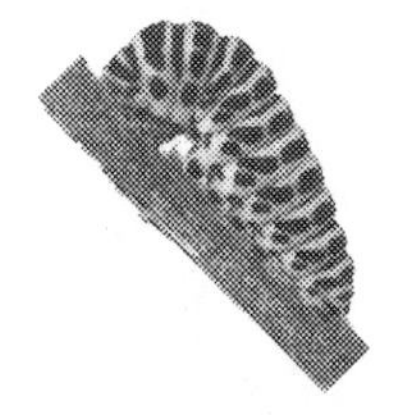

repeatedly--Buddha, Jesus, Buddha, Jesus...My mind was oscillating between Buddha and Jesus. In a split second, I opened my mind to Jesus when I asked this question,

"God, if you really hear me, I know you would reveal yourself to me."

Suddenly, I sobered up and began to think about my children who were still very young. How could I ever consider leaving them without a mother's love? It was so selfish of me to shirk my responsibilties as a mother to my children. They need my love.

On the spur of the moment, I had an unflinching determination of wanting to fight through whatever I was going through, and get back on my feet and continue living on in this world. I wanted to see my children grow up and become successful. I could not bring myself to leave them in the hands of others. It was my sheer determination of wanting to stay with my children that gave me the strength to refuse death and courage to live on. I needed God the most at that moment but I felt as though there was no god to help me when I needed him the most. I had no choice but to turn to Jesus to the rescue. HE was my glimpse of hope at that time. I clung to Him. HE granted me my salvation when I was spiritually dead. Benjamin continued sending me text messages incessantly to encourage me to accept Jesus Christ as my personal Lord and Saviour.

I needed God the most at that moment but I felt as though there was no God to help me when I needed him the most.

That was the most touching moment I had ever felt in my life. I was literally unconscious but mentally I knew I had decided to surrender myself to Jesus and told Jesus that if I ever woke up in the

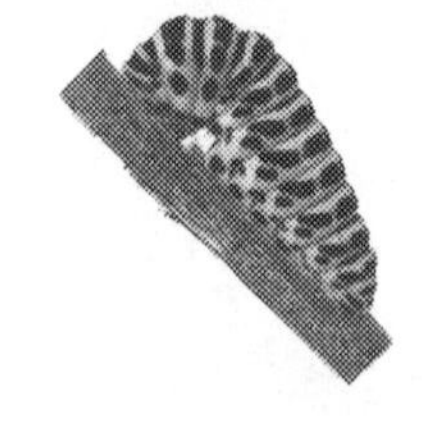

next morning being completely set free, I would declare myself to be the Lord's Child.

As I continued to call out to Jesus, I threw up and felt much better after that. I could not recall whether it was good long sleep or I was actually dead to the world. The next morning I found myself more alive than before with a renewed spirit.

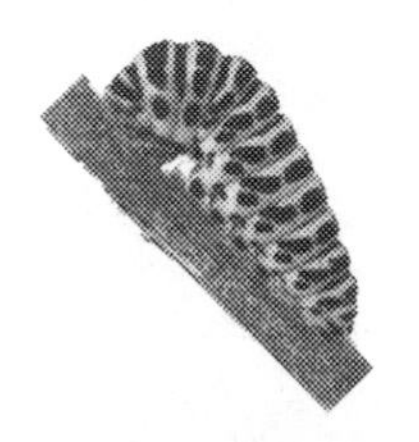

13

BENJAMIN'S MEMORY

Truth be told, at this juncture, I had given up on writing because I felt sick recalling the ordeal. But my friend Benjamin Sim sent me a long email with regards to what he could remember of that particular incident when we were exchanging SMSes with one another on my so-called Near Death Experience. I had been sending text messages to him incessantly in the midnights but due to insufficient storage space, he had deleted some of these messages from his mobile phone. This email serves as a motivation for me to resume my writing.

Benjamin's email:

I remember I saw your Facebook message stating that you were not feeling well and experienced a very scary situation as though you were going to die. That really shocked me and woke me up. So I thought I should sms you and asked you what happened to you. And thank God.

It was so good that you replied my sms and from there onwards your sms just came in non-stoppingly. At least three to four times in a night. Normally from nearly 12a.m. to 4:30 a.m. and also up the next morning onwards. And the second night, it happened again. So I just didn't know what to do and how to help you. So I just asked you to call out for Jesus for help. Just called out His Name and asked

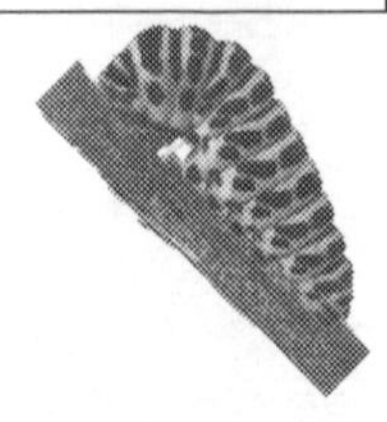

Him to come in to help you. Don't give up. Continue to keep asking and calling his Name. I remembered I told you that Jesus will surely help you. Have faith in Him. Praise God! It does help you a lot. But the thing just kept on coming back especially at night starting from nearly 12a.m. So in the end I told you no choice already. You have got to accept Jesus to come into your life and accept HIM as your Lord and Saviour. In that way I told you, it will be better because you are His Child now. You already accepted HIM as your Lord and Savior. He will come into your life wholely and fully and His Holy Spirit will also be in you to kick and destroy the evil one that is living in you. Hallelujah! At last miracle happened and you were free. Praise God! Thank You Jesus.

Benjamin's email on the retrievable SMS messages sent on the 11-11-09 (Benjamin wrote: I have deleted a few on the 9th and 10th and 11th) time 12.36am

> Tq. I need de most powerful Holy Spirit of God in de world 2 save my life. I hope that He is on his way. Jesus TQ very much. U hear my voice. Tq.

sent on the 11-11-09 time 8.44am

> I want 2 surrender myself 2 Jesus. I am very tired day after day. Im waiting 4 de time 2 pass so that I can find solution. What is your brother's number? How soon can i c him? Hopefully it's not too late 4 Jesus 2 help me. Tq.

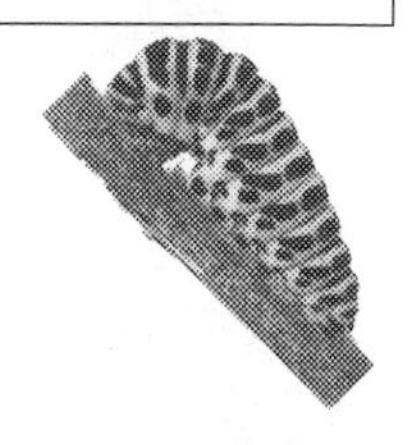

It so happened that morning my brother was not around, so I asked Mr Phan to talk to you. and he called you from Ipoh to talk to you and also led you to the sinner's prayer and guided you to accept Jesus as your Lord and saviour.

So it was on the 11-11-09 afternoon...that you accepted Jesus Christ as your Lord and Saviour...so that's the day you became a Christian...Hallelujah...Thank you Jesus.... and from that days onwards...there is no looking back. You Winnie Toh is completely free from all bondage and free from all satanic attack....Hallelujah!!.. the battle is won Jesus is so great. So now you are His Child.)

sent on the 11-11-09, time 3.33pm

> TQVM Benjamin. I'm now a Christian bcos I had no energy 2 struggle last night and called Jesus for help. Miracles happened. And I vomited out something when I called Jesus's name. Jesus has saved my life n I am Jesus's child. TQ Jesus.

I still remembered Benjamin posted some Christian CD's to me via courier as a blessing when I became a child of God.

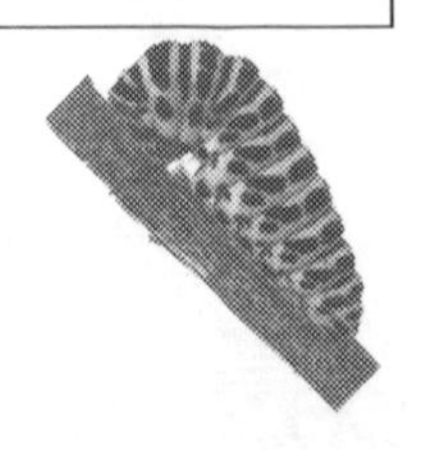

sent on the 11-11-09 time 5.48pm

> U r de messenger of Jesus 2 help me. Luckily I was open2 Jesus. Otherwise I would just surrender like that. Now i feel like I am reborn. The rest of my life, I live for Jesus.. Its quite tough 4 me 2 forget my previous religion but
> i guess Jesus is de most powerful God in de world 2 turn 2 during crisis. Tq...

The above is only part of your sms to me....and there are also a lot of my replies to you...which I can't really remember all of it... during that tough time..

It is on the 11-11-09 afternoon that you accepted Jesus Christ as your Lord and Saviour. So that's the day you became a Christian. Hallelujah!

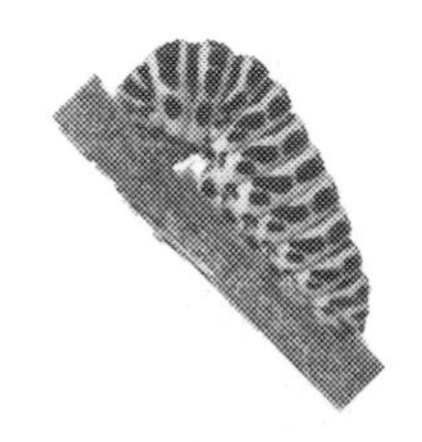

14

JESUS MY SAVIOUR

My side of the story was, in retrospect, in par with Benjamin's record of my communications with him through SMS.

After surrendering myself to Jesus on that night, I had a good night sleep finally, after so many restless nights. And spiritually I was renewed. I felt good being born again in Christ. It was quite tough for me to forgo my previous religion and practices. But I couldn't help being convinced that Jesus must have been the most powerful God to turn to in moments of crisis. He is my only Beacon of hope during troubled times.

Jesus must have been the most powerful God to turn to in moments of crisis. He is my only Beacon of hope during troubled times.

Lord, You are my refuge and my fortress, my God, in whom I trust. (Psalm 91)- this is the Bible Verse which reminds me of that tough time when I called out God for help.

The next morning, I felt rejuvenated.

I told Max that I had accepted Christ as my personal Saviour. He was not very pleased to hear that news but understood my circumstances and knew where I was coming from.

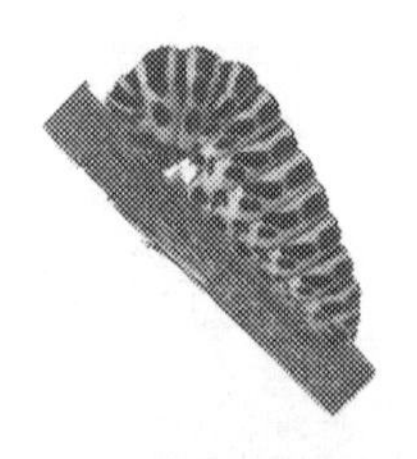

However, things did not seem to vanish instantly. The day after, I felt that my entire body from head to toe was being overtaken with by boiling evil blood. Matthew 12:45

It was back again. (Matthew 12:44)[1]

I had not repented of my sins yet. The acceptance of Christ had not been made complete.

"Where is Jesus? Did You not accept me. What had I done wrong that had caused flies to be attracted to the garbage?" I thought to myself.

My faith began to drop as I perceived that I was too sinful for Jesus to accept me.

I started texting Benjamin and asked him for help. He attended to my request quickly by attempting to locate a pastor or someone capable to help me to accept Christ into my life in a proper manner. He tried looking for his brother but coincidently his brother was out of town.

I was so desperate to hear from Benjamin. That was why I sent him the next text message.

---

1 Matthew 12:44-45 44 Then it says, 'I will return to the house I left.' When it arrives, it finds the house unoccupied, swept clean and put in order. 45 Then it goes and takes with it seven other spirits more wicked than itself, and they go in and live there. And the final condition of that man is worse than the first. That is how it will be with this wicked generation.

sent on the 11-11-09 time 8.44am

I want to surrender myself to Jesus. I am very tired day after day. I am waiting for the time to pass so that I can find solution. What is your broth- er's number? How soon can I see him? Hopefully it's not too late for Jesus to help me. Tq.

There were almost fifteen text messages that was being sent to Benjamin on 11 November. Since I needed help rather urgently, Benjamin made an arrangement for Mr Phan, a senior member from Lutheran church in Ipoh to guide me to accept Jesus as my personal Lord and saviour over the phone once again.

I followed Mr Phan as he led me in the sinner's prayer over the phone. He also prayed for my deliverance from Demonic forces and spiritual attack. As he prayed for me, he asked if I felt like vomiting. I did not respond. Eventually, he started praying in tongues. It did not happen until I ended my call with Mr Phan. I vomited.

At that instance, I felt set free from all bondages and spiritual attacks. 11-11 09 afternoon marked the date I accepted Jesus into my life officially.

I was in dire need of a Bible. So I called up a friend--Selina--to borrow a Bible, but I was not sure when I could get my hands on it. I was given Pastor Lai's number and was told that he was gifted in praying for deliverance. I also managed to attain a few other pastors' contact numbers through friends.

It was as if Satan knew my plan, and was trying really hard to stop me from meeting up with the pastor. I remember there was one occasion whereby I was wanted to drive out to meet the pastor when suddenly I lost control over my feet. It was then when I had a hunch that I was going to meet with an accident.

I even wrote in my Facebook like this:

> "I am driving to a church in about 10 minutes time... Appointment at 2:30 p.m.. Pls bless that I am protected by the holy spirit and able to meet the priest."
>
> 12-Nov-2009

I did not know how to differentiate between a 'Pastor' and a 'Priest' back then. I even made the sign of the cross on my chest (common practice of Catholics) as a protection against evil. My general knowledge about Christianity and Catholicism is poor as I was confused between the two.

There were many Christian friends who were following me in my Facebook and it was truly encouraging to know that they interceded and even conducted had group prayers for me. I felt that I was not fighting this battle alone.

There were many Christian friends who were following me on my Facebook and it was truly encouraging to know that they in- terceded and even conducted group prayers for me. I felt that I was not fighting this battle alone.

"You are in our prayers.. Jesus loves you and He cares for you.... May His protection and grace be upon you always... be strong and have faith in HIM. -Benjamin

When I logged onto Facebook to check my inbox messages, it was so touching that even a Facebook blogger called Ricky Soo in my network wrote a message to me the day before.

> Hi Winnie, I believe in your experience. It may be weird but it is real. 11 Nov 2009.

Yes I'm very concerned of your well being. If need help in anything can let me know, though I know not much I can help in your situation.

Ricky Soo then advised me to text Dr. George in K.L. to pray for me. I remembered I consulted Dr. George whether I should have a friendly discussion with the devil. And he replied in SMS.

12 Nov 2009

> Winnie, God asks you to fight, struggle and resist the devil! Not to have friendly discussion! Read Luke 4 and fight the devil like Jesus with the Word! He won so you also can win if you take him and holy spirit with you. My job is to pray for you and with you. I will! I have prayed and am praying now! Dr.George.

I thought I'd better ask for any pastor to visit me instead. But after dialing a few numbers, I noticed most pastors would prefer me to visit them.

I still felt the chills down my spine from my surrounding even in that afternoon itself. I was worried about my safety driving out onto the roads. I knew that I really needed help but I could not bring myself to step out of the house. So I tried my luck and I called Pastor Lai asking him for his favour to pay me a visit.

Literally, after getting the Bible I was racing against time reading the Bible in hope that I could be set free as soon as possible.

Surprisingly he replied, "No problem."

Hence, I cancelled my appointment at 2:30 p.m. with another church's pastor was cancelled and I was eagerly waiting for Pastor Lai's arrival.

When Pastor Lai arrived with his wife Christine, I felt really relieved and I could not express how grateful I was to both of them for making the effort to drop by and visit me.

After Pastor Lai and Christine prayed for me to be set free, he lent me a Bible. Literally, after getting the Bible I was racing against time reading the Bible all through the night in hope that I could be set free as soon as possible. I carried the Bible everywhere I went. It took me quite a while before I was completely set free. Pastor Lai and Christine also visited me regularly at my home to teach me the Word of God and prayed for me.

LESSON ON FORGIVENESS

I still remembered writing to a friend after my lesson on "Bitterness and Forgiveness" with Pastor Lai when I first accepted Christ.

Dear Sow Ying,

How are you?

I have converted my religion to Christianity recently. When the pastor asked me whether there is anyone in my mind that I cannot forgive in my life, I said 'no'.

However, when I was working on my book's forth printing in my printer's office, you appeared in my mind and Father told me to reconcile with you in order for Him to completely set me free.

I love Jesus and I am waiting for Jesus to set me completely free every single day. I just realised that my Heavenly Father loves me so much that he sent so many Christians to help me in producing my book in your organisation last time.

Actually, I have forgotten about the hatred or whatsoever between us. It is just that strong feeling sent by my Heavenly Father that I need to reconcile with you as my sister in the family.

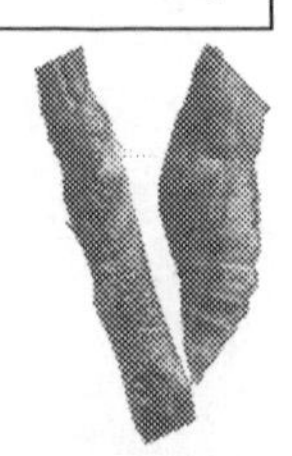

It would be nice to hear from you during Christmas. And may God set both of us free and let us enjoy this Christmas in the big family with our Heavenly Father!

Regards,
Winnie L.B..Toh

Dear Winnie,

Wow Winnie, this is the best Christmas present--to hear that you are my sister in Christ! Even though I have been a Christian for more than 30 years, I am learning new things from God everyday. One of the things that touched me now is the fact that God loves us so much and He also wants us to love one another. I am also learning the power of forgiveness to lead a happy and healthy life. Would really like to catch up with you to know more about your spiritual journey.

Sow Ying

Sow Ying was prompted by God to write an email to me a few years back when we had some misunderstanding. But the fact that I was deeply hurt, I was not ready to reconcile with her during that time.

How great is the Lord! He prompted us to get in touch with the person whom we think we are hurt by. We all think we are the righteous when we have misunderstanding with others. And most of us will wait for the other person to ask for forgiveness if we want to reconcile. It does take up a lot of courage to ask for forgiveness from the other person because we will lose our pride for doing so.

Sow Ying was prompted by God faster than me to ask for forgiveness as she wrote in another email:

"God has been revealing to me that unforgiveness is damaging not only to my soul but also to my body. So I have decided I will do my part whatever the outcome and be obedient to Him."

I used to think only Buddhism teaches about 'forgiveness and forgetting'. But our Lord teaches even more. In Matthew 18:21, Peter thought he was generous enough to let his brother sin against him for up to seven times for most of us allow a maximum of 3 times. But Jesus answered not 7 times but seventy-seven times which represents infinity. He gave us the hardest commandment i.e. to love your enemies.[1] For most of us, it takes time to heal the bitter- ness before we agree to reconcile but our Lord teaches us to reconcile immediately.

---

[1] Luke 6:27 "But to you who are listening I say: Love your enemies, do good to those who hate you..."

BUTTERFLY WITHOUT WINGS

The story has not ended yet. I was a butterfly but I could not fly. Truth is I was yet to be set free.

When Pastor Lai and Christine came for a visit, I was delivered from the oppressions in my life through their prayer. But after a day or two, the enemy would return, usually during a certain hour at approximately 2 a.m. in the midnight.

Had converted to Christianity really helped in disentangling from the problem? Eventually yes. In my case, the deliverance was not a one-time event. It was a process that God was working in me. One thing for sure was there were many followers of Jesus standing in to help me in my times of need.

Pastor Lai texted me. In fact, he was the person I turned to whenever I was assailed by Satan. I was not sure how many text messages had I sent him especially in the wee hours. Despite of the time, he replied me almost instantly every single time.

> 'Read John, The Word of God. The evil spirit is afraid of it.'

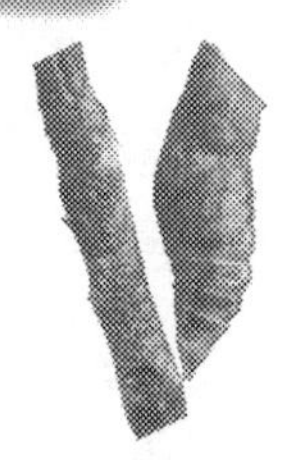

I felt rather guilty having had to bother Pastor Lai in the witching hour of the night with incessant text messages. To my astonishment, he was ever ready to help me and to pray for me.

At times, the attack was so severe that I just felt that one Bible was not sufficient to protect me. I felt many needles pricking my body that I literally wished I could lie on many Bibles in hope that they will "protect" me and relieving me from the discomforts. I had this niggling thought at the back of my mind about it coming back. Sometimes I felt like I need an antidote for it--I was being foolish. God has given me His Spirit and the Holy Spirit is able to work miracles. Yet I chose to believe my own perception.[1]

As I did not want to interrupt Max's sleep. To assuage my anxiety, I usually moved to the balcony in our masterbed room quietly switched on the light and read the book of John in the Bible. As soon as I started reading this book, I felt countless numbers of evil spirits fled from my body.

God had been reaching out to me by sending his disciples to guide me and to speak the Word of God to me. The Bible was my only solace in those difficult moments and the Word seemed to stand out whenever I read it. At times, I broke into tears because the presence of God was overwhelming to me.

I did not know what and who came next but I knew that God was sending me good samaritans every single day to help me go through

---

1 Galatians 3:1-2 1 You foolish Galatians! Who has bewitched you? Before your very eyes Jesus Christ was clearly portrayed as crucified.
2 I would like to learn just one thing from you: Did you receive the Spirit by the works of the law, or by believing what you heard?

the ordeal I faced. I remembered attending a service the whereby Pastor Chee preached a message on the topic 'Spiritual Warfare' and he taught us to utilise the word 'bind'.[1] It was as if Lord was speaking to me through the sermon, preparing me against the wiles of the enemy.

Christine-6/12 sms

Today's message in church sounded like revision for you. God's word continues to dwell in your heart. God Bless.

The enemy started attacking my thoughts via 'mind attack'. I started to get some false signal of illnesses resulting in my mum and relatives being really concerned. I recalled my mum calling me in the midnight to find out if I was alright.

I was suspected to have had Typhoid, Thyroid, blood circulation blockages or whatsoever ailment--you named it. Some people suggested that I should go for health check-up. In attempt of proving that I was perfectly fine, I went to two check-ups with Pathlab and the Adventist hospital.

Some of my non-Christian friends and relatives were trying to brainwash me back by asking me to change my mind. Some commented that I did not look for help thouroughly enough and it was a hasty decision that I would later on regret.

---

[1] Mark 3:27 No man can enter into a strong man's house, and spoil his goods, except he will first bind the strong man; and then he will spoil his house.

I still remembered my sister-in-law whom I seldom got in touch with suddenly called me up one day because she was concerned about me after stumbling upon some of my postings in Facebook which were posted awhile ago.

She picked me up for a drink and we chatted about the incident. "I am a neutral person. Since you have chosen to accept Christ, I respect your decision. But do you want to go for another health check again? Perhaps a Chinese physician this time. I can go with you just to ensure that you are free from Thyroid. You know, Thyroid is very common amongst women. I will bring you there later."

I accepted her offer and went with her. But the Chinese physician was not around.

My mum was beginning to grow anxious about my situation. She went everywhere she could just to pray for me. And she even suspected that I might have contracted this debilitating disease which could possibly cause death. So much so that my mum arranged for my cousin to prepare some traditional old wife tale's medicine to apply all over on my body.

Truth be told, I felt really sceptical about all these rituals carried out. Rubbing ointment on my body, throwing raw rice all around my house to name a few. Nonetheless, I accepted their act of kindness shown to me and permitted-them to do whatever they will just so they could feel better. Secretly within me I did not care if it would affect me- My faith is indeed in Jesus alone. Out of respect sake I gave in to the many suggestions given--But from the core of my heart, I knew Jesus is the only true living God--who could truly heal me.

Facebook

Would like to plan for a trip to K.L. on Thursday if I am recovering. Tomorrow I am arranging for a blood test to check for my health condition. Next Wednesday, I have another appointment for a thorough health check- up. I am trying every method to get back to normal condition- psychologi- cal, scientific, religion, etc.

16 November 2009 at 7:04 p.m.

Praise God! My medical check-up from Pathlab results proved that my health condition was normal. No Thyroid or whatsoever suspected diseases.

My next action plan was to go for spiritual healing sessions done through the power of my Lord.

Inside me I only had Jesus, the one and only true living God. I put all my trust in HIM that HE is the one who could heal me.

A few Christian friends of mine contacted me via private messages in Facebook and gave me some useful contacts that could be of assistance to me. Stephen Tong was one of them who asked me for my phone number so that his wife Kimara could give a call me to see if she could be of any help.

I still remembered Kimara taught me the word 'rebuke' over the phone. Apart from that, she also reminded me about getting to the root of the problem in order to solve it.

I wrote Stephen an email on 14 Nov 2009:

Facebook Inbox message:

Dear Stephen,

Where is your church in KL? In case I go to KL, I might want to stay in touch with my Father by going to the church.

But first I must be completely 'set free' by Jesus in Penang. Then only I can plan for my KL trip.

My Bible is 'Sunrise Good News Bible' - lent by Pastor Lai who is following up with my case.

Do pray for my good nite sleep bcos it is not over yet. There are a lot of hindrances but I am still persevering in search of my one true Father.

TQ. God bless you!

Winnie

Dear Winnie,

I am happy to note that you are really growing and learning fast. My church location is at http://kts-isaac.net/location.htm

Always praying and journeying with you.

Now your brother in Christ,
Stephen Tong

As I was unable to find a solution to the problem, Stephen Tong and Kimara had arranged for me to meet up with their pastor, Pastor Michel Wright in Kuala Lumpur for counselling.

Both Stephen and Kimara were very hospitable. They came all the way to pick me up from the KTM station, and sent me to the church on the 30th of November. I did not know them that well yet at that time, as I only communicated with Stephen a few times through Facebook. But deep in my beart, I knew that God's people are always trustworthy. I had a feeling that our Lord will continue to arrange many more different messengers to guide me along my journey.

We went for a drink before the appointment with Pastor Michel from Kingdom Transformation Sanctuary - ISAAC.

MEETING WITH PASTOR MICHEL WRIGHT

"How can I help you? What have you been going through?" Pastor Michel Wright asked.

"I don't know, really. I just participated in a Beauty Pageant Contest and encountered with what seems like demonic attacks." I replied.

"Pastor, we thought we'd bring her here to see you to see if you can be of any help. She comes all the way from Penang." said Kimara.

"I have just accepted Christ and I still feel something pressing against the pulse of my head." I explained.

"Oppression, you mean?" he asked.

"Yes," And I went on to expounding the whole matter stemming from the Beauty Pageant Contest to Pastor.

"It felt as though every night at a particular time the idols which I used to pray to, come back. Sometimes I dreamt of the Goddess getting very angry. I was struggling to fight for a peace of mind." I exclaimed in frustration.

"Look, this is a spiritual warfare. When one encounters with a problem, he goes and looks for a bigger 'God' to help him. After helping, the 'God' wants to exchange something. Then a bigger problem arises, he then goes and seeks for a stronger spirit to help him. In the end he has to come to Jesus." Pastor Michel reassured me.

"Your idol is just like your lover. He comes back at certain hour to check whether the house is empty. If your faith in Jesus is not strong, he can easily come back."

"Now listen to what I have to say to you. You have already had God's word embedded in you and nothing can enter you. You must always remember this. Now, repeat these words after me...."

He opened the Bible and read aloud some Bible verses and requested me to follow after. I looked very weary as though Satan was blocking my mind from receiving God's words. Pastor Michel began to purge my mind according to God's word.

"Do you understand what I am trying to tell you?" he asked. Pastor Michel then gave me a list of ten statements to meditate and confess everyday on top of reading the Bible so that I can proclaim Christ who is living in me.

THE TEN THINGS YOU MUST BELIEVE AND CONFESS TO YOURSELF:

1. **YOU HAVE ETERNAL LIFE**
   There is NO reincarnation.

2. **YOUR SINS HAVE BEEN WASHED AWAY**
   You do not need cleansing all the time, just confess your sins to Jesus and they are washed away.

3. **YOU ARE COMPLETE IN HIM**
   There is nothing you lack or need when Jesus is IN you.

4. **YOU ARE MORE THAN A CONQUEROR**
   This means no sitiuation can conquer you because of Jesus within you.

5. **YOU HAVE A SOUND MIND**
   Since Jesus in IN you your MIND will always be at peace and you will not worry much.

6. **GOOD HEALTH IS YOUR INHERITANCE**
   Jesus's PRESENCE within you will ensure that your body is well provided you take care of it.

7. **YOU ARE THE TEMPLE OF THE HOLY SPIRIT** GOD lives IN you so you do not need to run from church to church to find him.

8. **YOU CAN DO ALL THINGS**
   Through Jesus who lives in you.

9. **GOD'S POWER WITHIN YOU IS MORE POWERFUL** than any other power around you, so do not live in fear.

10. **REVELATION WILL FLOW FROM WITHIN YOU**
    You will not need to search for answers outside, God will speak to you from his Spirit within you.

MEETING WITH DR. CHIA

13 Dec sms

> Good evening. Pls be reminded to come over and collect your Wellness Report tomorrow. Thank you!- Adventist Wellness Centre.

I returned back to Penang and made an appointment with Dr. Chia, the Medical Officer (Wellness Center) of Adventist Hospital to analyse my medical report.

"Good. Your medical report is overall satisfactory." he announced. I was given a clean bill of health.

Dr. Chia then went on to suggest ways I could do to improve my health.

"Do you know how can I get my brain scanned? I feel as though something is putting pressure on my head. Do I need to see a neurologist or a psychiatrist?" I asked.

There I was, repeating the cycle once again. After countless counselling sessions, I still did not fully grasp it.

"When God's Word is in me, no other spirit will enter me."

That was the exact statement Pastor Michel said to me. Truth is, it was easier said than done. I did have faith in the God's Words but somehow I could not stop feeling the oppression on my head.

"What makes you worry about whether your brain is functioning well or not?" Dr. Chia asked out of curiousity.

With God's prompting, she suddenly asked me what made me go for the medical check-up and whether there was anything worrying me about my health.

"I feel a kind of oppression happening very regularly. I think I just accepted Christ and have not really gotten things over yet." I expressed in desperation.

"Praise the Lord! I am also a Christian. I tell you what, you do not need to see a neurologist. Let's see how I can help you. I want to listen to your story of how you came to accept Christ. Come back at 3 p.m. and I want to see you on this."[1] Dr Chia said.

Wow! Father. I was so amazed that God sent another disciple of Christ to talk to me to help me to get through the odeal. A doctor was taking her time out for me. I was truly blessed.

I was anxiously awaiting to go to Dr Chia's clinic at 3 p.m. When I arrived, I was still wondering whether she really meant it. Perhaps it was a consultation session which I had to pay.

---

1 1Peter 3:8 Finally, all of you, live in harmony with one another, be sympathetic, love as brothers, be compassionate and humble.

Yes. She was prepared to see me. When I went in, she was all prepared to hear my story.

And so, I told her my entire story. And she told me her opinion at the time I was encountering demonic attacks before accepting Christ, the holy spirit inside me was not equipped enough to fight against it. And in name of Jesus, we need to build up our faith and believe that all demons are under his feet.

She explained to me a lot about the Bible and the truth. She also told me a few stories of new believers encountering the same kind of demonic attack. Whether it is human quarrels or spiritual attacks, one may still come under attack hours, days or even weeks later-. even after finding freedom in Christ. We should continue walking in faith with God, resist the devil and he will flee from you.[1]

She prayed for deliverance for me. I felt as if Jesus was speaking to me through her. Her sincere offer to see me in a special session, her sensitivity to listen to me and her prayer truly touched my heart. Dr. Chia even gave me her mobile phone number.

"In case you need help, you can always call me." she said.

How privileged I am to be called a child of God, being attended to by a doctor who is also His disciple.

After seeing her in a long session, I asked the counter for the consultation fee, and true enough, it was free of charge for me.

---

[1] 1 James 4: 7 Submit yourselves therefore to God. Resist the devil, and he will flee from you.

MEETING WITH PASTOR MICHEL WRIGHT

Some of my non-Christian friends or relatives felt betrayed when I told them that I had accepted Christ and left my old religion. Amongst those were my aunts who thought that I was supposed to be a good mother, looking after the kids. Why did I suddenly go for what Beauty Pageant Contest and switch religion? And Max's family background is strong in ancestral worship and accepting Christ would be very contradictory to that belief.

"Do you really think that Christ is your only way out?" that was the typical question my aunt asked.

"Yes. He was with me when I needed HIM the most," I answered. "Why made such a hasty decision? You should have asked for help from us!"

How ironic of the likes of them to say that. It was easy to offer help when things were over. The time I really needed help, people were too busy and the ones who paid attention to me were God and God-sent messengers.

God has perfect timing for everyone. When it is time for one to accept Christ, he will cry as if he is touched by God.

God has perfect timing for everyone. When it is time for someone to accept Christ, he will cry as he is touched by God. I would never forget that wonderful emotional feeling when I received Christ. Tears of sheer joy streaming down my cheeks and the presence of God was so real at that very moment.

Most of the time, people finally found God in times of real crisis. In my case, this was how I found God.

I have observed that there are many seekers who take a long time to analyse Christianity. They have been sitting in the church for years to investigate the truth of the Bible and to decide whether Christianity is the right path for them. Many are still wishy-washy and waited for many years to get baptised. Some still want to put off baptism until they are really clear of their directions.

Jesus saved you and you should become a Christian.

In my case, I did not wait long to analyse whether Jesus is the real living God. Jesus came to my Saviour at the right time, I did not have any worry what the future holds for me in the Christianity journey. Without Jesus, I would have perished.

I was a living testimony to those non-Christians who saw how I went through my ordeal and accepted Christ. They blessed me in my journey in Christ. Although my mum is not ready to accept Christ yet, she always says,

"Jesus saved you. You should become a Christian."

I could tell that my mum had tried ways and means to save me but she had surrendered her daughter in the end to Jesus Christ.

20

THE TONGUE LANGUAGE

4 Dec 2009

I recalled receiving my tongue language over a dinner table prayed by a church member during the Emma FNC Anniversary.

Over the dinner table, I heard one of the church members singing in a foreign language. At that time, I did not have a clue what tongue language is. To me, it is similar to Buddhists chanting mantras. When people chant, they chant in another type of language. The only difference is that Buddhist chanting is book-based and needs to be learnt by heart whereas Christian tongue language is a gifted Heavenly language. Glossolalists speak unlearned languages freely with the gift from the Holy Spirit.

At that time, I did not have a clue what tongue language is. To me, it is similar to Buddhists chanting mantras.

"Winnie, would you like to receive tongue language from theLord?" a church member asked me.

"Over here? Are you sure it works?" I asked in confoundment.

"Why not? Let me pray for you. But first you must desire the tongue language and invite the Holy Spirit to teach you."

She prayed for me to receive tongue language. Then asked me to follow her uttering,

"Dah Dah Dah Dah...."

"O.K. you are just like a baby now learning how to speak. You do not need to struggle on your own. The Holy Spirit will move within you. Be patient, it will come naturally."

Suddenly, I burst out speaking in tongue. I was bubbling nonstop as if I was speaking with a supernatural power.

"I felt like--" I was groping for the right word to describe how I felt.

I felt as if I needed not have to strive hard to speak in tongue. I was like an expert speaking in another foreign language like Hindu or African.

I recalled I was overjoyed when I knew how to speak a new language. I remembered consulting Stephen about the tongue language in Facebook.

5 Dec 2009

Dear Stephen,

Just curious. Is every Christian gifted with the tongue language? Does the words have any meaning?

Why am I talking like an expert? I entertained my baby with the tongue language and he was so amused by that. He mimicked me by playing with his tongue when he saw me doing it. It's so cute.

Can we use it anytime like while driving in the car, playing with the baby, etc. or is it only meant for communicating with God?

TQ.

Winnie

Act 19.6,,,, etc. Tongue language== heavenly language.

Dec 2009

Dear Winnie,

Every Christian will be given the gift of tongues if they have a DESIRE for it. It is a GIFT..

Remember, Pastor Michel told you from the Bible that, "--No one can proclaim that Jesus is Lord except with the help of the Holy Spirit."

The tongue that you have received is the PRAISING TONGUE.. it is your spirit combined with the Spirit of God (the Holy Spirit) inside you praising God and confessing that Jesus is Lord in the heavenly (spiritual) language.

Yes you can use it any the time you want to--so that your spirit together with the Holy Spirit will keep praising the Lord.

Next, you also desire to ask God to give you the understanding of what you are speaking. Just keep quiet after you speak in tongues.. The Lord will speak to you--This is to help you GROW to the NEXT level OK? [:)]

For your homework, read the following passage. http://www.bible gateway.com/passage/?search=1+Corinthians+12&version=NKJV

Do let me know if you have further questions.

Have a blessed day,

Stephen

21

THE VISIT FROM LUTHERAN CHURCH, IPOH

8 Dec 2009

It was a surprised visit from the Ipoh Lutheran Church members on 8 Dec. They came in a van led by Pastor David. Mr Phan who is a senior church member was amongst them.

Words could not express how touched I was by the love and care shown by these followers of Christ--they travelled miles from Ipoh to visit me. It was very magnanimous of them to give part of their precious time to visit a stranger like me. It made me feel that in the Lord's family, we are all brothers and sisters. Moreover, knowing that it was impossible for me to be a member of their church, they still travelled all the way from Ipoh to visit me. Among the many denominations in churches, I felt that this church has the most caring disciples of Jesus who have pure hearts of wanting to help people without expecting anything in return.

They began singing Christian songs that were not just soothing to the ears. Their songs reached my soul--and warmed my heart. Amidst the singing, we felt the strong family bond. The neighbourhood was

surrounded with the House-Visiting wassail, so as to speak. Then, they shared testimonies with me to encourage me to continue to walk with Christ. Pastor David helped to pray over the oppression on my forehead by anointing with olive oil.

It was an eye-opener for me as this procedure required the elders of the church to pray together as one.[1]

It is believed that the prayer offered in faith would cast out devils. I was slain in the spirit and experienced 'the falling phenomenon'--(an event when a person falls to the floor and has a personal encounter with the Holy Spirit, often associated with the practice of laying hands on the person.)

I was supported by a few people from behind to prevent me from falling down backward to the floor. I regained my balance after 'resting in the spirit' momentarily.

Not long after, Pastor Lai and Christine came and joined us for networking. We had Penang Hawker Food and Rose's homemade cream puffs as dessert. It was all arranged on an impromptu basis.

Those were the first few times I joined the Christians for meals together. I was not used to praying before meals. But it was very disciplined of the Christians to pray before every meal.

---

[1] 1 James 14: Is anyone of you sick? He should call the elders of the church to pray over him and anoint him with oil in the name of the Lord.

Christians' prayer before meals:

'Our heavenly Father. Thank you for bringing us together as your family. Bless this table of plenty. Thank you for the abundance you have given to each one of us. Nourish our souls as well as our bodies, so that we may always be mindful of those who are less fortunate than we are, so that we may go forth into the world to feed those in need. Amen.'

As a new Christian, I had been struggling on how to pray. But I had the desire to thank God for his provision of food. Normally, I shorten the prayer before a meal.

'Thank you Father for the food, Amen!'

I was inspired to write the following song from this chapter to motivate brothers and sisters of Christ to stay united as a big family.

Song

We are one family in Christ -Winnie L.B.Toh

Key: C major

Verse 1:

```
C         F              C
We are one family in Christ
F                                        G
Together we hold our hands and sing
              Em                  F
Though we don't know one another
           C              F
There is no barrier in us (pause)
           G
Let our love manifest
                 C
The Glory of God
```

Verse 2:

```
C         F              C
We are one family in Christ
F                                     G
Together we pray and grow in love
  Em      F
United we stay
     C             F
For all the world to see
        G              C
We are one family in Christ
```

Chorus

```
   F                          C
Oh Father! Teach us to forgive and forget
   F                          C
Oh Father! Teach us not to fight
F                       C
Help us to forget the bitterness
   F                        G
For we are living in your name
                  G               C
End: For we're one family in Christ
```

Bridge

```
F                Am  F          Am
We are one family we are in Christ
F                Am  F          Am
We are one family we are in Christ
Oh Jesus….
```

22

MEMORIES OF CHRISTMAS

As Christmas drew near, accepting Christ rekindled my long lost memory of Christmas in England. It used to be an occasion I looked forward to when I spent my eight years in England. I recollected the nostalgic memory of Christmas carollers singing Christmas songs with guitars in front of Sainsbury in London. The most memorable lyrics that stayed in my mind till now are "Silent night, holy night…" and "Jingle bell, Jingle bell, Jingle all the way…" As the day becomes dark very fast during Christmas time in England, the only entertainment we had was listening to Christmas Carols and admiring the sparkling Christmas street lights in London.

I recounted those years during Christmas we used to visit my aunt and uncle in Peterborough. We had a cosy Traditional Christmas Dinner cooked by Aunt Nancy. Turkey, Yorkshire pudding, roasted sweet potatoes, sprouts and Christmas pudding. We would then exchanged presents with one another.

Once we went for a drive in my brother's rented Smart car to Sandringham in Norfolk where the Queen and the Royal Family used to spend their holiday there.

I recalled visiting Sandringham during Christmas to see the British Queen and Royal family members making a public appearance for the traditional Christmas Day church service at Sandringham. We went there on a separate occasion. I met The Queen, Prince Charles, Prince William, Prince Henry and all the other members of the family on that day. During every Christmas, all the well-wishers who wished to greet the Royal family woke up very early in the morning and drove to Sandringham to await for the arrival of the Royal Family. If I were still there today, I probably would get a glimpse of The Duke and Duchess of Cambridge--Prince William, Kate Middleton and their son Prince George. But I guess I have refrained from idolatry after I have become a Christian. The one who deserves my idolation is Jesus. He is the promised Messiah. He died on the cross for our sins, He heals the blind, He casts out demons, etc. He is all powerful God. On his robe and on his thigh he has this name written, "King of Kings, Lord of the Lords."

This year Christmas really made a difference to me. I felt I was coming home to celebrate with my father Jesus.

I have been celebrating Christmas over the years but I never thought of Jesus. In Malaysia, I do celebrate Christmas but in different ways.

Christmas this year really made a difference to me. I felt that I was coming home to celebrate with my Lord Jesus. Although there is no biblical proof that Jesus was born on Christmas Day, Jesus is the reason for the season.

TESTIMONY IN A COFFEE SHOP

Things seemed to calm down for a few days. On 21 December, I received a call from Pastor Lai inviting me to give testimony on Christmas Eve in the church. Feeling hesitant, I rejected the offer initially as I wanted to put an end to the ordeal as things seemed to be back to normal. In another words, I did not want to find trouble again.

Pastor Lai's SMS dated 21/12

> Winnie, you will be fine because you are lifting up the name of Jesus. HE will protect you. Do not be afraid. Go ahead with faith. He will strengthen you. We will pray for you. Remember--Lord Jesus who is in you is greater than the devil who is in the world. Amen!

It was like God was calling me and it was hard for me to say 'No'. Reluctantly, I agreed to testify. On 24 December, about an hour before I started my journey to the church--I felt oppression and nausea coming on me heavily--I almost gave up going to the church. It was then I realised that the enemy of the Lord has attacked me.

Pastor Lai prayed for me as soon as I had texted him.

Pastor Lai's SMS dated 24/12

> James 4:7-8 quotes- Submit yourself to God. Resist the devil and he will flee from you. Come near to God and he will come near to you.
>
> Revelation 12:11- They overcame him (devil) by the blood of Jesus and by the world of their testimony.
>
> Confess these words to yourselves first. When faith arises, command the devil to leave agreesively in private.
>
> We will also pray for you. Do not be afraid, God is on your side. He is protecting you.

I did not know how long it took to conquer the oppression and nausea, but I remembered feeling lighter when I finally arrived at the church, safe and sound. It was as though the enemy and everything evil associated with him flee at the sight and presence of the Holy Lord. Thank God for that!

When I reached there, Pastor Lai reassured me that I was fully protected. I was composed in time and soon got myself engrossed with the activities of the day. It was just about one or two items more before the sharing of testimonies began. All of a sudden, the electricity tripped in the middle of the celebration.

Call it coincidence or what, but I believed firmly that it was a spiritual attack. I felt the eeriness surrounding during that time--having a hunch that something untoward would happen on that night. Until that night, the electricity had never tripped in the church during Christmas eve. It sounded too far-fetched given what had transpired.

The church was shrouded in darkness. It could be due to a short-circuit case but the power was cut out of the blue. Feeling relieved that I needed not have to give testimony, I thought the party was destined to be called off. There was nothing we could do about it except wait to go home.

Just as I was about to excuse myself and go home with the kids, Pastor Lai and Christine directed everyone to move to the coffee shop downstairs. We groped our way down the dark staircase with the help of our mobile phone flashlights. Soon, everybody was evacuated from the building.

Not long after, everyone started to work together to arrange the chairs on the street. Performers started to stand in the space facing outside of the coffee shop. They started to perform on a platform with two steps above as if they were on the stage. It was a great arrangement, lickety-split. Thanks to the wisdom and creativity given by the Lord to His people. Soon the celebration became lively. It really made everyone feel like Christmas listening to Christmas carols accompanied by guitar playing.

Feeling relieved that I needed not have to give testimony, I thought the party was destined to be called off.

We were honoured to have a Filipino vocalist to sing to us.

Even though it was his debut performance, he sang wonderfully well. Soon, there was an announcement that it was Testimony Sharing Time.

I started to have butterflies in the stomach. Not because of having to stand in front of an audience but rather have to find my courage to share my testimony. There was a church member sharing her testimony before me. Not having to present testimony first somewhat eased my tension. As soon as her testimony finished, it was my turn. I did not expect to give the testimony in a coffee shop. Be that as it was ordained, I did it. I decided not to wory about fum- bling and failing that time. After all, Christmas was never about me. Nothing could stop us from celebrating Christmas and ultimately testifying for our Lord Jesus Christ on that important day.

OUR FATHER'S HEAVEN

Not long after I accepted Christ, I went to a MPH Bookstore branch and browsed through some books. From far away, the title of a book under the 'Christianity' section caught my eyes--'Heaven is so real' by the late author Choo Thomas. I felt like the Holy Spirit was guiding me to walk towards the book and pick it up. It was an international best seller book. It tells an extraordinary story of a Korean woman being taken by the Lord to visit Heaven for thirteen times.

I started to flip through a few pages and the Bible verses of the book stood out as if the Lord was talking to me.

Without any hesitation, I just grabbed the book and paid for it. I was intrigued to know what exactly our Father's Heaven is like. When I arrived back home, I could not stop reading page after page of the book. The next day, I was so enthusiastic to carry on reading the book--trying to find out what Heaven is like, what we eat there and what pleasure we can have in Heaven.

'In my Father's house are many mansions: if it were not so, I would have told you. I go to prepare a place for you. And if I go and prepare a place for you, I will come again, and receive you unto Myself; that where I am, there you may be also' (John 14:2-3)

At times, I broke down into tears when the Bible verses in the book touched my heart. It was as if the Lord was talking to me. I felt that He was trying to show me what His Kingdom of Heaven is like through that book.

I will never be righteous with the Lord as human has sinful nature. If I were to analyse Christianity before accepting Christ, this will be the main reason for me to accept Christ.

I finished reading the book within two days and was very excited to share it with some Christian friends. I could feel the Lord talking to me whilst reading the book so much so that the words stood out and made me cry intermittently. Do I believe her testimony? Yes. I believe that when certain supernatural experiences are shared with worldly people (unspiritual people), it is hard for them to believe it. In fact, they might think that you are insane or psychotic. But if we share with people with the same experience, we can empathize with each other's real encounters. Late Choo Thomas was just sharing what she had experienced. Although some parts of her story were beyond belief, no one is in a position to criticise as the Lord taught us not to be judgmental.[1]

I believe in Heaven. Without a shadow of a doubt, I know that it is real. It is my dream to go to Heaven when I die. The greatest achievement in life and beyond life is to end up in Heaven. But Heaven is too perfect for everyone to enter. I know that I will never be righteous with the Lord as humans have a very sinful nature. If I were to analyse Christianity before accepting Christ, this will be the main reason for me to accept Christ--we will never be perfect and deserve to go to hell. But our God is so merciful and loving that He does not want to see many perish-- He understands our imperfections can never reach his

[1] Matthew 7:1 Do not judge, or you too will be judged.

Holy nature, thus he sent our saviour Jesus Christ to this world to die for our sins so that we may have eternal life.[1] We are saved by God's grace. We just need to have faith in HIM that we will be saved.

My children have been asking me to describe what Heaven is like. Since a picture is worth a thousand words, I showed them the pictures from Google image online. They are too young to understand the meaning of salvation and eternal life. To illustrate to other children about Heaven, I simplified the description into a poem suitable for children from four years and above.

---

[1] John 3:16 For God so loved the world that he gave his one and only Son, that whoever believes in him shall not perish but have eternal life.

Sunday School Poem:

Heaven

-Winnie L.B.Toh

Heaven is real
Till it's revealed.
What can we see?
Please tell me.

The Angels sing,
Glory to the King!
Streets of Gold
That's what we are told.

Flowers, animals and streams,
Whatever in your angelic dreams.
Make sure we are in the Book of Life
To see the beautiful river of "river of life".

If you enter the Kingdom of light
You will be alright.
For He who did sacrifice
Brings His children to His paradise.

NEW CHRISTIAN HELP

I still remembered asking Ricky Soo (http://facebook.com/ rickysoo) a few questions when I first accepted Christ. I had no general knowledge about Christianity at all. I was either unobservant or ignorant. Imagine I did not even know what 'Amen' means during that time.

> 19 November 2009 13:19
>
> Dear Ricky,
>
> Hi, just to consult you on the following:
>
> 1) Do we have to say 'Amen' when we pray to Jesus Christ? Does 'Amen' mean 'agree'?
>
> 2) I am not baptised yet. My mother asked me to observe a few churches first before committing to one church. She said some churches will ask you for never-ending donations.
>
> 3) Actually I would like to commit to my pastor's church because he is the one who helps me the most. But I want to hang on to being baptized first. I can do something for them in return for a period of time but I want to choose a church which is nearer to my house.

(Acknowledgement to Ricky Soo for the permission to use the facebook address.)

This church of mine--they use the word 'Amen'. My mum said 'Amen' is a newly created version of Christianity. Thank you for your enlightenment-- Brother. Winnie New Christian

20 November 2009 08:32

Hi Winnie,

Sorry for the late reply.

1. "Amen" means "so be it". It is not "agree". It is standard and biblical. There are a number of instances in the Bible as per http://www.biblegateway.com See the Lord's prayer in Matthew 6:9-13 and the footnote at the 'Keyword Search' tab on the left-hand side of the webpage. Amen is there. There is no fixed and hard rule what to say in prayer. Saying "Amen" is a tradition we follow because our Lord Jesus did so.

2. There is no hard and fast rule which kind of church to attend. It's up to your personal preference whether to attend church in a shop lot or a landed property. The important thing is that church teaches the right way of Christianity, serve God (not serve the pastors), and accountable to members for its fund, among other factors. Donation (called tithing in Christianity) is something between you and God. Don't be compelled to "donate" too much or too little. The tithe is for God's purpose in churches so that more people come to know Jesus. There are a number of "denominations" in Christianity.

But it's O.K. because all are serving the same God, only stressing on different aspects.

3. I encourage you to attend to the pastor or the church you are with now and pray for future direction along the way. There may come a time God asks you to change churches. Let God lead you. You just focus on now.

20 November 2009 11:02

Dear Ricky,

1. Amen- So all Christians use the word 'Amen'. Then I should follow.

2. There is a Baptist church in front of my house--two minute walk from my house.

3. For the time being, I will serve the church I am with now because the Pastor is really good. He comes to my house with his wife to teach me the Bible and be my helpline even at midnights for the past few days. Slowly, as what you say, I need to pray for future direction from the God because my pastor's church is very far from my house. Recently, my friend from K.L. told me over the phone that it is O.K. to go to whichever church we are comfortable with. She goes to different churches every week. Until now she still has not been baptised although she has been a Christian for many years. I am getting better and better every night. Last night, I was able to sleep with 'some' of the lights off. Thank you for the guidance.

Winnie

I was not an observant non-believer before accepting Christ. One will be surprised that here were the few things I was completely clueless about then:

1. Imagine I did not know the story of the Fallen Angels, where Lucifer a.k.a. Satan and his supporters rebelled against God and was cast out of heaven, hence this story also commonly referred to as the War in Heaven.

2. The Fall of Man, the Adam and Eve's story of their first sin.

3. In Christianity, we are descendants of Adam and Eve, not a biological evolution from apes as Darwin's Theory of Evolution had suggested.

4. To be honest, I did not know about the denomination of churches until I consulted Ricky Soo.

5. I have come across the term 'Trinity Church' before but did not know the meaning behind it, i.e. The Father, the Son (Jesus), and the Holy Spirit; one God in three persons.

6. I heard about Easter but shame on me. I did not know what the Pentecost (occurs 50 days after Easter) is and why the Holy Spirit is released.

7. There is indeed a lot of jargons that I did not know of. I did not even know the exact meanings of 'salvation', 'holy spirit', 'deliverance', 'God's grace', 'hymns' and why Christians say 'Amen' and 'Praise God' all the time.

Thankfully, my Christian brothers and sisters did not just leave me alone after I was saved. They have been edifying me since then until now with the Word of God. I attended 'New Believers Bible lessons' by Pastor Lai, and other supporting classes on the Christian culture such as Baptism class, Discipleship class, Masterlife, Cell group and Bible discussions. I had learnt a lot from mature Christians.

...If a new believer is saved and not guided, he will remain a carnal Christian and will not grow spiritually.

I would say if a new believer is saved and not guided, he will remain a carnal Christian and will not grow spiritually. A big 'thank you' to all my older Christian brothers and sisters for holding my hand to walk with Jesus!

THE WATER BAPTISM

I was so eager to get baptised during Christmas in 2009. But Max was not ready to accept it. Out of respect for him, I waited until the following year to get baptised. It was five months after I accepted Christ that I was officially baptised--still considered very fast for a new Christian. Since there was no turning back, what was I still waiting for?

4 April 2010

It was Jesus resurrection day in Easter. God was so good that He arranged for Max to be away in Kuala Lumpur when I had my water baptism. I did inform him and explained to him that there was no turning back for me and I hoped he would respect my decision.

It was a beautiful Sunday afternoon--a happy occasion for me. After the Sunday sermon, we all went to Pastor Lai's condominium at Gold Coast. It was very supportive of the church members to witness my water baptism. My two kids were there to witness mummy being baptised in the swimming pool. Well, they did not know anything at their ages, they just tagged along to have fun in the pool.

I was blessed with a picturesque resort to get baptised. From afar, I saw a seemingly immaculate swimming pool with scenery of coconut trees swaying in the gentle blowing wind from behind.

The water looked turquoise and crystal clear. I brought along my swimsuit to change and just before we walked to the pool, I was surrounded by the church members and they prayed for me.

I remember Pastor Lai asking me some questions to ascertain that I was not being forced to be baptised. It was all on my own free will.

I was all ready to go forward for the baptism. We proceeded to the swimming pool. Pastor Lai and Christine were in the pool waiting for me.

Just before I went down the pool, I was asked to give a speech.

Winnie's Speech (-recorded in *youtube*)

"Today is the day I get baptised into Christ. In the Chinese Calendar 4/4 means 'die' that is to be baptised into Jesus's Death. My husband knows that I am baptised today but he is in K.L. I told my husband that I cannot wait for him anymore because the end time is coming. I don't want to wait until everybody is rushing to be Christians and the pastor is too busy to entertain me. Many of my friends who are Christians are still not baptised yet. In the Bible, Mark 16:16 it says, "He who believes and be baptised will be saved." In Acts 22:16, "Why are you waiting? Arise and be baptised. Wash away your sins". I am ready today."

The audience burst into laughter on and off when listening to my speech. Without turning back, I ambled towards the swimming pool as it were walking the aisle on my bare feet towards Pastor Lai and Christine.

Winnie's Baptism 4/4/2010

Pastor Lai asked me three questions of commitment. It was all 'Yes' from me.

I nodded my head. Both Pastor Lai and Christine then held my hands and back. I was asked to squeeze my nose with my fingers.

"I baptise you in the name of the Father, of the Son, and of the Holy Spirit," declared Pastor.

There I went, being plunged into the water backwards, was fully-immersed in the water and being raised up to a standing position again.

I was delivered.

I heard applause and was overjoyed. The angels in Heaven must be rejoicing over one sinner who had repented.

The kids were excited to play by the pool after the ceremony was over. They were frolicking around in the pool and we had a whale of time there. We visited Pastor Lai's unit and chatted before we left.

How did I feel after being baptised?

I felt that I had no more connection with many disguised demons in this world forever scheming to poison our souls and minds. Praise God! I was completely set free. I am filled with the Spirit of God and my sins were washed away.

I felt as if I had turned from a jaded, wingless butterfly into a radi- ant butterfly with fully functional wings. Jesus had repaired my broken wings and I was restored, renewed and I could fly high through the rains and winds.

I felt as if I had turned from a jaded, wingless butterfly into a radiant butterfly with fully functional wings. Jesus had repaired my broken wings and I was restored, renewed and I could fly high through the rain and winds.

All my recurring problems of satanic attacks were completely gone after getting baptised--as readers can find out in the latter part of my story that there is no more darkness in my life. It was as if I had crossed over to the light of the world. And this time, it is for real. I was completely cut off from my former connections.

Baptism was the best solution for me to declare publicly that I am married to Jesus, the bridegroom of His people. And at last I was able to partake the Holy Communion[1] in church after baptism--a prerequisite for taking the Lord's supper.

---

1 Holy Communion- an act of remembrance of Jesus' death. Bread and Wine/grape juice are used as the elements of communion. Bread symbolises the body of Christ. Wine represents the blood of Jesus. In His Last supper with His disciples, Jesus told them to do this in remembrance of HIM.

THE WORSHIP TEAM

It was not long after I was baptised that I received the gift from the Holy Spirit to play by ear. I was able to sense the highest calling from the Lord to play the keyboard as my fingers had been moving at midnight as if I were playing the piano. The calling to worship team resonated within me. I felt Him gently asking me to place my fingers on the keys and play according to His direction He impressed upon me. The melodies that came out from the piano were discordant at some parts, but I did not mind. When the Lord moves in you so resolutely, the last thing you want to do is deny and hold back. Doubt displeases the Holy Spirit, and God cannot work wonders with his faithless believer if the believer ceases to believe in Him.

It just so happened that Pastor Lai was planning to train up a keyboard player to back up his son Reuben--I was more than happy to help out.

Back then I had no idea of how to play any worship songs. All I was given were titles of the songs and I needed to search from You Tube to gauge what chords and keys to use.

It was a challenge for me for a start. At first, I complained about no notes being given. How on earth was I able to pick up new songs within two to three weeks as I was all new to Christian songs and had not much time to practise everyday?

I was quite clumsy when I first started. Firstly, I was only used to the piano and was not familiar with the keyboard and its complicated functions. A piano and keyboard look the same and it should function similarly, but I soon realised the keyboard has different sound characteristics than a piano. The way you move your fingers across a piano and a keyboard is different too. Secondly, I did not know how typical worship team works. When a worship leader decides to change the key in the middle of a song, the keyboard player has to accommodate fast. I was very bad in transposing the keys and identifying the order of tones and semitones.

God chooses the unquali- fed to do his work. So when we accomplish, the glory will go to Him and not to us.

In the corporate world, an employer would generally choose an employee with the right technical qualifications to do the employer's job. But with God, God chooses the unqualified to do his work. So when we accomplish the work He sets before us, the glory will go to Him and not to us.

Thank God, Reuben was very helpful. He was very talented in keyboard and had been in the worship team for more than ten years. I remembered I was in awe of Reuben's talent in playing the keyboard. Basically, his song sheets are clean. Unlike me, who have to scribble many notes down so that I do not forget the way a song should be performed, Reuben does not even bother to write down the chords for reference.

When asked how he improvised so many extra notes in it, he told me there are not many tips except to play by feelings as he flows by playing around with the chords.

Reuben wrote me the chords and I was able to incorporate into it. Slowly, I was able to fill in extra notes in the songs by feeling the presence of the Holy Spirit guiding me.

I was given the chance to play the keyboard all by myself during worship time. Praise God! I breezed through each time. Although I was not happy with my performance, still the mistakes were not obvious as the singing voices were loud enough to cover my mistakes.

During the free worship time, I felt my fingers dancing on the keyboard spontaneously. If people asked me how to play those melodies, I really could not answer because I just played by feelings that washed over me that time. Those feelings never repeat in the same music twice.

I remembered I love to record my songs and uploaded them on You Tube. One of the songs with the highest number of viewers is "Come Holy Spirit fall on me now." To me, it was not played perfectly but someone requested for the song sheet by writing this to me:

"That was really a good arrangement that you performed. I play ed the piano as a beginner so I depended on the notes. God is good He gave you that talent to play it by ear. I was hoping if you have written down note by note then I can play it on the piano in church."

After replying I was only played by ear, the person wrote back again and said,

"Hi Winnie, is there a way I can request a song sheet from you even if I have to pay for it?"

Indeed, I really did not have notes to share because it was all played by ear. Before I became a Christian, I did not know how to play by ear. The songs I played were based on notes and printed materials and they were very rigid. I find Christian songs are creative and very flexible. There is space to add in beautiful variations as the Holy Spirit leads. The Play-by-Ear Skill was gifted by the Lord. All glory goes to HIM!

I am still not a good keyboard player--for I cannot sing and play at the same time. When I start singing, my keys are all jumbled up. What is more, if I do lead a worship session, I cannot multitask and do three things at a time. Praise God! I did it more than once in my cell group. I could do it. God gave me the strength to do it. I am still improving myself but at least I am far better than I was before, as I did not have these skills before I accepted Christ.

1 Exodus 35:10

"All who are skilled among you are to come and make everything the Lord has com- manded."

When I changed church, I knew being in the worship team was no longer God's calling as my fingers had stopped moving fluidly in the midnight.

God had a new plan for me. It was His prompting that I exercised my other skills i.e. writing. But then again, I was unqualified to write a Christian book during that time. I could feel that He equips me to do it from time to time.

Youtube:
Come Holy Spirit fall on me now--Winnielbtoh

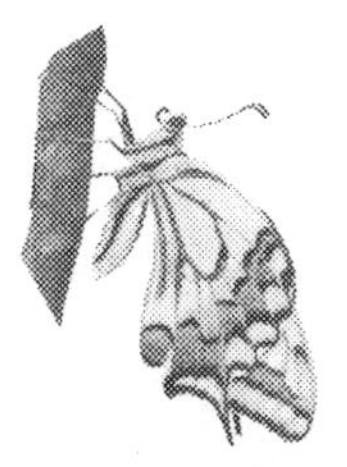

Worship Song

Key: Bb major
Unqualified **-Winnie L.B.Toh**

Bb Dm
Unqualified, we're the chosen one
Eb F
Lord, you choose us for your purpose
Dm Eb
You are there, Holy Spirit, Lord
F
To guide us accomplish your work

Bb Dm
Unqualified, we're in Your favour
Eb F
You, qualify the chosen one
Dm Eb
You'll equip us with extra skills
F Bb
Let the glory be to our God

Pre-Chorus

Bb Eb
Glory glory glory be to our God
Bb F
For without You, there is nothing we can do

Chorus

Eb Bb
We humble ourselves under your mighty hands
Eb F
You will exalt us in due time
Eb Bb
We trust You Lord, we will be anointed
Eb F
And we thank You Lord for using us

Bridge
F major

Dm C Bb
You make it possible…. Possible
Am C
For the impossible
Dm C C Bb
We thank you Lord, We thank you Lord
Am C Bb Am Bb C
For making us special

28

THE NEW HOUSE

It was after I was baptised that the attacks on me came to naught. In fact, the demon took the action to a new level and shifted attention to my other maid and other members in the family. In other words, there was no more attack on me but the other members of my family encountered spiritual attacks.

I always heard stories about my maid being attacked at night. Whenever she encountered the attack, she would complain to us the next day.

Now and again, she felt like a lot of demons surrounded her bedside. My mum taught her the old wives tale of putting keys besides her bed to scare away the spirits but the Legion was too powerful to be driven away. During bedtime, sometimes she felt the demons on top of her that she could barely move her body and was unable to scream.

We heard stories of noises coming from the recycling bags at the back of the room and the scuffing of slippers in the kitchen area during the wee hours. We also heard stories of the kitchen light being switched off suddenly and when my maid was alone, she could feel a shadow besides her.

During the Hungry Ghost Festival--the Chinese version of All Souls' Day--we heard the remote call bell for dinner in the house playing music at midnight without anyone pressing it.

At one time, she was filled with trepidation. We were at our wits'end of helping her to solve her problem. So we took her to the church to see the pastor. When Pastor Lai prayed for her, it appeared like something fled from her body and she looked scared. Jesus has the authority to put Satan under His feet. And He does it for anyone who asks Him for it. During that time, she nearly converted to Christianity but something seemed to hinder her from doing so.

Despite the obvious spiritual troubles the non-believers had experienced--and Christians had helped to deliver them from their troubles--it does not guarantee the delivered non-believers will accept Christ after witnessing His power over demons. Doubt and Fear won over my maid's heart then. Doubt held my maid back from truly seeing Christ as He is, even though she was fully aware she was attacked spiritually. Fear of possible rejection and persecution from her family, relatives and friends was more powerful than the power of salvation she had experienced in the Lord's presence then. Come to think of it, I believe that Doubt and Fear are spirits. They grow when we feed on them more instead of feeding on Jesus' Word, or at least positive things to believe in. Doubt and Fear can unwittingly grow to be great weapons for the Enemy to use against us.

I supposed receiving Jesus at that one moment in time is easy, but Life goes on. So how does one go on in Life but is ill-prepared to deal with the changes? I could only hope in time, my maid would learn the true strength and will of the Lord for her, and that is the Lord would want her to have a life of true peace and joy abundantly, a life where no enemies on earth, Heaven or Hell can steal it from her.

My eldest son was also a regular victim of the spiritual attack.

He was always admitted to hospital almost every fortnightly for being sick. When he had high fever, he would tell us a lot of stories of him seeing things that our earthly eyes cannot see. Once he said he saw a scary 'Red Dog' wanting to kill him.

Finally, I believe God intervened and the Lord knew what was best for us. We were only staying in our house for two years plus and the house was still brand spanking new. But for some reasons, Max wanted to move house again. It was also time for us to start looking for a new house within spitting distance of my children's school. So, we started looking for houses.

We had upgraded to a better house and I thanked the Lord that He had reserved this dream house for us. It was one of the first few houses we saw around two months back. After two months, we could not find our ideal home and we decided to purchase this house and surprisingly it was still available for sale.

I love my new home very much. It is very suitable for hosting a cell group meeting or a Christian fellowship gathering. The peaceful environment and conducive work space are also very suitable for writing and composing songs. I believe the gift comes from God and He has wonderful purposes for me in this new home.

We finally find peace in the new house--no more hauntings, no more Red Dog threatening my son, and no more spirits burdening my maid. Thank God for the blessing.[1]

---

[1] Jeremiah 29:11...For I know the plans I have for you," declares the LORD, "plans to prosper you and not to harm you, plans to give you hope and a future.

My quiet time with the Lord in the new house

THE NEW CHURCH

The Lord continued to bless me with a life of Riley in my new house. I cannot express how blissful I am to be gifted with this new house. It was time for me to make a decision whether to leave EMMA Faith Nurturing Centre or to stay.

At first, I felt really guilty of changing church---for Pastor Lai and Christine had helped me to go through my journey as a young Christian and to endure the ordeals in it along the way. It was very ungrateful of me to leave them and go for a bigger church near my house. I left the worship team as well. Actually, I had already told Pastor Lai that I might have a change of direction of church in the future. I guessed they were mentally prepared for it. The main reason for me to change church was I needed a church in close proximity to my house which can provide me complete spiritual growth e.g. prayer meetings, sermons and cell group meetings.

The Lord reviewed to me that it is not quite right to attend two churches-- for one cannot serve two churches at the same time.

Although I sometimes joined the Truelight Baptist church in Mandarin service which is near to my old house for convenience sake, the Lord reviewed to me that it is not quite right to attend two churches--for one cannot serve two churches at the same time.

I remembered writing this on my Facebook wall posts:

Torn between Two Lovers

The wall posts attracted a lot of attention but for those who know me well or are discerning, they read between the lines and figured what I meant---I was torn between the two churches.

The Lord found me a solution. By moving house, I left my two churches and started anew with another church.

Changing church was a good test for me to see if my focus is on the Lord or human. If I remained at EMMA FNC because Pastor Lai had helped me before, my focus was not on the Lord but on human.

I continued to pray and seek for Lord's guidance on which church is suitable for me and what he wanted me to do next. There are two churches near my house--Wesley Methodist Church and Georgetown Baptist Church (GBC). The formal one is nearer to my house.

Somehow the Holy Spirit guided me to visit GBC first. As soon as I stepped in, the staff were very welcoming. They took down my particulars and did the follow-up. I even received a welcome letter by post signed by Pastor Kok Aun to welcome me to join GBC. I was invited to the sermons, prayer meetings and cell group meetings. And on top of that, I had the privilege to have one-to-one Bible lesson with Jane on every Wednesday. How blessed I am and I had found my spiritual home and did not feel like leaving GBC from the first day I stepped into GBC.

Life had been wonderful at the turning point of my life with the blessing of my new house and new spiritual home i.e. Georgetown Baptist Church. But my membership still remained with EMMA FNC until the day I felt the need to change to GBC. I would probably transfer my membership a year after in order not to hurt Pastor Lai's feelings. Thank you Father that Pastor Lai was very understanding. God had a better plan for me at GBC.

Not long after I joined GBC, I was excited to perceive that GBC was in the pipeline of building a new building just besides the church. How blessed I am to be part of the family.

The new church is my motivation to complete my book. Whenever I groaned about the hard journey of writing this book, I would compare my challenge with that of building a new church. Surely to construct a building is far harder than anything else. The team involved must have perseverance to achieve their goal. Imagine they started ten years back to plan for this new building. The actual building work started sometime in July 2012 which was about the time I started to further develop my book. Whenever I was bogged down with my writing project, I was encouraged by the new building. Whenever my project was postponed, I would comfort myself that there was no rush to complete because GBC new building completion date had also been postponed from 2014 to first half of 2015. If the team members involved are persevered enough to wait for the completion, so am I! I believe if we do not give up, one day we will reap a harvest.[1]

---

[1] Galatians 6:9 (ESV)
"And let us not grow weary of doing good, for in due season we will reap, if we do not give up.

THE CALLING TO WRITE

I was in a quandary about my direction after moving house. During my quiet time, I sought earnestly for the Lord's calling.

In time, I felt a strong prompting that the Lord wanted me to write my story.[1] It appeared to be paradoxical as I had this fear of being a writer again. Ever since I published my books and board games, I swore to myself I would never ever write any new books in my life. To me, the process of publishing a book is tough.

When I went through the new believer kit with Jane to renounce my sin of swearing in the past, I did recall this incidence of restricting myself from publishing another new book by making a vow. After renouncing this sin of making a vow, I felt the prompting to sit down to compile my story. I had a strong feeling that the Lord was trying to say that this writing experience will be different and my past experience will be put to good use this time. I cannot afford to be selfish any longer and keep the testimony to myself..

As soon as I made the decision to write this book, I had Mr Phan from Ipoh in my mind to edit my book for me.

---

1 John 15:27 And you also will bear witness, because you have been with me from the beginning.

I texted Benjamin to ask him to find out whether Mr Phan was willing to edit my book for me. To my amazement, Ben told me that Mr Phan was with him and he had said 'Yes'.

In the past (when I was a non-believer), finding an editor for the other book written by me was not that easy. I went to the extent that I cried out to God to help me find an editor. It took me a long time to find one.

But in this project, it was smooth sailing. I found an editor just like that. This was how I discerned God's call. When it is God's work, he will provide whatever we need.

This was how I discerned God's calling. When it is God's work, He will provide whatever we need.

The Lord had arranged for Benjamin to travel to Penang from Ipoh for business trips. Each time he came to Penang, I would pass the manuscripts to him. I did not even need to worry about how to get the manuscripts to my editor because of the travelling distance.

It just so happened that my tuition centre partner decided to organise a field trip to the butterfly farm forour school holiday programme. I took many photos of the butterflies supplied by the Lord.

I believe it was his arrangement for me to help out with the librarian work on a monthly basis so that I am exposed to more Christian books.

I started with compiling my stories from tracing back my Facebook posts from year 2009. I was then preoccupied with teaching classes and children. I had almost forgotten about revisiting my book. Once I

went online to make inquiries about publishing a Christian book from an International Publishing Company. Ever since then, the publishing consultant did the follow-up very regularly by writing and calling me from overseas. I was not serious enough to sign up with them but each time when I was approached, I was reminded about my unfinished work.

I was also energised by Benjamin when each time he said he was going to come up from Ipoh, it reminded me about passing him more manuscripts for him to take back to Ipoh.

Lord, forgive me if I discerned you wrongly for asking me to write. But since I am already into it for You, guide me and give me the inspiration and wisdom to complete the project to glorify your name!

Ben motivated me to look into the graphic designing work of the book when he asked me whether I needed him to source for graphic designers for me. Besides, Mr Phan also forwarded me a sample book cover designed by a graphic designer in Ipoh. But I decided to advertise online to look for suitable graphic designers for the interior of the book. And my mail box was filled with many applicants for two to three weeks. Even after a year, there were still enquiries for the job.

This was when I felt that by publishing this book, inadvertently it created more job opportunities around. Besides, I am giving a chance to graphic designers to develop a book to gain the experience.

As this is a Christian book, I could not simply cherry pick any graphic designer to design the book in particular the book cover. All inspirations must come from the Lord. That is why for the book cover, I engaged Inspiration Hub which is a Christian based publishing firm to do it.

I had been praying for wisdom from the Lord to choose who to engage in this project and I trust that it is His plan to engage certain people to take it to the next level.[1]

As time passed, I realised that publishing of this book was for real--no ifs, ands--or buts about it. It is a pain to go through the process of developing a good book. Towards the final stage, I gave up at least half a year to focus on God and His words for more input to write this book by joining the Bible Study Fellowship and Masterlife course. At the same time, our cell group had also decided to do a special Bible study based on a book. I trust that it was His arrangement as coincidentally my students were cut down during this period after I had made up my mind to take a break. The year 2014 seems to be the year of accelerated Biblical studies for me to equip me with writing my book. Lord, forgive me if I discerned you wrongly for asking me to write. But since I am already into it, please Dear Father, guide me and give me the inspiration and wisdom to complete the project to glorify your name! If You are the one who began the work within me, I believe You will continue Your work and help me to finish the race.

---

1 James 1:5 If any onf you lacks wisdom, he should ask God, who gives generously to all without finding fault, and it will be given to him.

31

LEARNING HOW TO PRAY

I still remember not knowing how to pray eloquently was my main concern as a young Christian. As Emma FNC is located very far from my old house, I did not join the prayer meetings which are held during night time. I recalled writing this on my Facebook wall post.

Facebook 5 Mar 2011

> Learning how to pray makes me feel like a baby learning how to speak-- lack of vocabulary, shy, afraid of people listening to me, etc. Time flies. I've been a Christian for a year but still do not know how to pray. I shall not let this problem persist. Otherwise, after 10 yrs or 20 yrs down the road, we're still talking like babies. How embarrassing!

My insecurity and doubts about not being able to come any closer to God was a terrifying fear, I mean, when you fall in love with someone who means the world to you, you would do anything to get closer to him, respect his revealed secrets and know what pleases him.

I was like a blind woman desperately trying to grope for doors of opportunity in the dark, hoping it will lead me to another level higher, closer to God. The only solution to that prayer, something I was afraid of buut I cannot deny it is the necessary road to reach out to God. I had not known then that God already knew my heart-felt wishes before I even utter it out to HIM. So, when we do not know the right word to pray, the Holy Spirit intercedes for us to pray in accordance with the will of the God.

After coming across Roman 8:26-27[1] in my Bible, I said a humble request to the Holy Spirit,

"Oh Holy Spirit, help me in my prayer life by giving me utterance in prayer, guide me to pray in accordance to God's will. In the name of Jesus, I pray. Amen!"

In a span of a few days, there were already nineteen comments in response to my Facebook post dated 5th March. I remembered my Facebook virtual friend, Matthew Leow, suggested this on 9th March:

> Matt 6: 9-13 is a good format to follow on how to pray

Aside from that, I still remember having a long debate on Facebook with a Christian friend of mine named Orpheus who insisted that Christians should be given the liberty to pray in their own ways. It is not important to have the same pattern in praying. Prayer comes from one's own heart, for God has created each of us to be uniquely different.

Orpheus wrote:

> You are the very first person I ever met in my life--either before or after I have become a Christian who usually sticks to certain particular references from verses of the Bible as so-called the correct, or even the best wordings to pray.

---

1 Roman 8:26-27 In the same way, the Spirit helps us in our weakness. We do not know what we ought to pray, but the Spirit himself intercedes for us with groans that words cannot express. And he who searches our hearts knows the mind of the Spirit, because the Spirit intercedes for the saints in accordance with God's will.

He added:

It is easy to realise God will definitely listen to everyone who prays with a true and honest mind, in a humble manner, whole-heartedly. But the message within is more important; not any brilliant and fancy statement.

I remembered this statement made by him:

What is the criteria and grounding for you to choose those whom you think as a good reference for praying? Doesn't it really matter to ask and even insist everyone follow the content within?

Orpheus even kindly shared with me a sample of his prayer of that day:

6 Mar 2011

My dearest Father,

Another sleepless night! Just recap on how and what I have done to hurt so many people whom I met in my past forty years' life span which made me deserve the current loneliness status. I think this situation will last till I kneel down on the judgment of my very last moment on earth. Lord, heal me, forgive me and hug me unconditionally--to ease my pain, release my guilt, comfort me for what I had been suffering. I must confess my sins, truely and honestly. Thereafter, hope I can start to taste and lead an eternal life, if and only if, I am being authorised and blessed to so. Therefore, I can stay in a sin free but full of love and joyful paradise. Hope I am the one to be made parted of the amazing grace of being a blessed sinner.

Amen.

Not long after, this friend of mine from Hong Kong passedaway in his forties.

I still remembered when the news of Orpheus' death came down the pike, I could not believe what I heard. I wrote to his sister to confirm the truth.

From : winnie Toh <winnietoh21@hotmail.com
Subject : Hi
To : ivywong917@yahoo.com.hk
Date : 2011 8 31 8:30

Dear Ivy,

This is Winnie here from M'sia. I recently logged into Orpheus's Facebook and got a shock from his wall posts.

Has he really passed away? What happened to him?

May he rest in peace in Heaven. Amen!

TQ.

Winnie

In the end, she wrote back to me this:

Date : Wed, 31 Aug 2011 23:00:46 +0800
From : ivywong917@yahoo.com.hk
Subject : Re: Hi
To : winnietoh21@hotmail.com

Hi Winnie,

Yes, Orpheus is now in Heaven due to an accident.
Can you share here the good memories of him or any photos, etc. or remembrance?

Thanks for your email and God bless!

Ivy (Orpheus's 2nd eldest sister)

Farewell to my friend. The Lord had answered to his prayer. My last communication with Orpheus on the 'Prayer' topic on my Facebook will be forever enshrined in my heart. We debated on this topic with endless postings and private messages in Mar 2011. How could I ever have foreseen that he would go home with the Lord so soon?

To a Christian, death is the beginning of eternal life with less suffering. Oh Orpheus, enjoy your eternal life in Heaven and our Father will give you a good hug and you no longer have to suffer in the worldly life.

This testimony has proven that the Lord actually hears our prayers. If one prays fervently with his heart, the Lord will answer his prayers.[1]

The beginning of my prayer life brought to mind that my spiritual mentor, Jane, who always encouraged me to pray together with mature Christians in public prayers to listen to the way they pray.

What is amazing about Jane is that most of the time whatever she prays for, the Lord will answer her prayer. At least her intercessory prayers for me were all being answered. I see it as she is so righteous that I can find no fault in her. That is why whatever she asks for, the Lord hears her.[2] Even though not hundred percent He answers the righteous, He hears their prayers.

---

[1] 1 Samuel 16:17 The Lord does not see as a human being sees; human being see only the outward appearances but the Lord sees into the heart.

[2] Proverbs 15:29 NIV, "The LORD is far from the wicked but he hears the prayer of the righteous.

As a beginner, I learnt how to pray by following a simple acronym of praying i.e. ACTS

1. Adoration - praise HIM for who He is
2. Confession - confess our sins and ask for forgiveness
3. Thanksgiving - we thank God for the many things he has done for us
4. Supplication- submit our prayer requests to God

As we grow, the Holy Spirit will guide us to pray in many ways. I remember I used to be intimidated when I sat together with mature Christians. I had this fear of letting them hear my prayer in public--I was too self-conscious about that.

Slowly, I improved and I can pray better in public now. There are times when we spend quiet time with the Lord to pray alone[1] and there are times when we do corporate prayers. Christians do intercessory prayers for others as well. When Christians grow, they seldom pray for themselves or they learn to cut down "shopping list" of personal prayer requests to God. Instead, they do intercessory prayers for the country, nation, add fasting to their prayer lives-- among those prayer warriors are the ones who go for 7/24 prayer movement, Global Prayer Network, etc.

When I have a heart-to-heart talk with the Lord, sometimes He does answer to my prayer if I really seek for HIM.[2]

---

[1] Matthew 6:6 But when you pray, go into your room, close the door and pray to your Father, who is unseen. Then your Father, who sees what is done in secret, will reward you.

[2] Luke 11:9-10 Ask, and it will be given to you; seek, and you will find; knock, and it will be opened to you. For everyone who asks receives, and he who seeks finds, and to him who knocks it will be opened.

If my prayers are not answered, I learn to accept that my prayers are not according to God's will.[1] Or that God will answer my prayers at a later time.

Praying is part of a Christian life and we are expected to pray regularly. An example of a disciplined Christian daily prayer routine should be at least an hour in total- if you feel you can add in more time to it, why not? Everyone leads a different live depending on his job position in the corporate world and at home but the breakdown of the general routine could be as follow:

A Christian's Daily Guide to A Consistent, Prayerful Life

Morning (upon rising): Devotion time--Pray for about 20-60 minutes. Wise prayer warriors find that quiet time with the Lord works best at 3-4 a.m. As for me, my quiet morning with the Lord is upon waking (around 7:30 a.m.) to be still before Him, and start the day with God..

Devotion time: pray

Breakfast: Pray for blessing of the food. Around 10 seconds or less.

Day time: marketing--Before going to work or do household errands, commit to the Lord for safe commute journey and good vibes for a positive atmospheric day to work at office or home.

---

[1] Isaiah 55:8-9 "For my thoughts are not your thoughts, neither are your ways my ways, declared the Lord. As the heavens are higher than the earth, so are my ways higher than your ways and my thoughts are higher than your thoughts"

Lunch time/afternoon: Pray for the blessing of the food. If you have some extra time alone before/after lunch, you can pray longer and commit whatever worries you have in mind to God, i.e. children's school activities, exams, major domestic or business decisions, healing for someone, etc.

For those can hardly find time to pray, consider praying during driving. Many Christians find prayers for parking spaces effective and for me God answers my prayer everytime.

Dinner: Pray for the blessing of the food. When having fellowship dinner, no need long list of blessings. The people's hungry stomachs around the table would really appreciate you for that.

Night: If attending prayers meeting--- pray for church, commu nities, nation, government and international issues.

Night time (before bed): Make a thanksgiving prayer, praying for salvation of the family members or friends (P/S: to non- believers: like it or not, your Christian friends do pray for you. The persistent ones might have been praying for ten to twenty years, or a lifetime till their dying breaths).

For new baby Christians and busy working Christians, it is a challenge to come before the Lord when there are endless tasks begging you for immediate attention, but you knew the Lord should come first somehow. The Holy Spirit prompted you on it. But how to do our daily responsibilities and spend time for God without falling dead tired from the hectic rush of life?

According to a pastor, in order to not feel daunted by praying for an hour a day, one should start small first, say 5 minutes a day. Within that 5 minutes, block off every form of distraction trying to get to you. Nothing should come between you and God within those 5 minutes alone with Him. Once you can settle yourself peacefully within that 5 minutes time frame, you can add on another 5 or 10 minutes next week or so. As time goes by, you would notice that you inexplicably want to spend more time with God, so adding time to your usual daily devotion time with Him would be automatic. It is not recommended to spend, say 60 minutes, on your first daily devotion attempt. If one sets for a goal too ambitiously high, chances are that he may end up disappointed.

When your first try-out did not yield the results you expected, you may be demotivated to do anything for the Lord after that. Accept the fact that a towering tree does not grow overnight--the same goes with prayer life.

For an unanswered prayer or making important decision, fasting and prayer might go hand in hand to have a deeper fellowship or relationship with God. If what we ask for brings glory to Him or is according to God's will, He will grant us our prayer request. Many mature Christians do fast. It is biblical--not compulsory but something we are encouraged to do.

God chooses the unqualified to do his work. So when we accomplish, the glory will go to Him and not to us.

A consistent prayerful life takes time to nurture as a habit but it undoubtedly sets a strong foundation between you and God. It sounds like painful hard work but one will enjoy the hard work and wonderful rewards he would gain from cultivating a sturdy relationship with the Lord.

THE CELL GROUP

I had a refreshing memory of my first time joining the Cell Group from Damansara Utama Methodist Church (DUMC). I recalled telling Aaron Toh about needing prayer when I was in K.L. He invited me to a Cell Group Meeting at the Cell Group leader's house.

It took an hour to drive there, to--a meeting place in someone's house situated in Petaling Jaya. Being my faithful chauffeur--as readers have read in previous chapters that he fetched me all over Malaysia--Max was kind enough to fetch me there. He waited for me at Starbucks nearby.

My first impression of joining the Cell Group was that the Christians there are blessed with a sincere, warm-hearted sense of fellowship that abounds plentifully. The promise of many rich, fulfilling friendships from DUMC church members are high. I felt welcomed into a large family where I no longer have to worry about loneliness when I grow old. As I am aware of my growing age, I do yearn for rewarding friendships with good Christians. Meaningful relationships does make life beautiful indeed. It can change us in many ways, and one of them is that the presence of good friends in life makes you less depressed or afraid of Death.

Before I reach that part of life later, I have hoped by that time, I have touched so many hearts that some would remember to pay their last respects to me at my funeral, be it believers or non- believers of Christ. For a Christian, if one joins a Cell Group, even for the wake service of immediate family members of the Christian who are non-believers, the Cell group members support

Coming back to my story on DUMC, as soon as I stepped in as a visitor from Penang, the DUMC church members were welcoming although they knew that it is unlikely for me to join them as a member in the future.

We sang worship songs, played some fun games and shared testimonies. That was an eye-opener for me as I had always wondered what Christians do in their meetings.

Then, we started the Bible lesson as revision on last Sunday's sermon. It felt like going back to elementary school days, studying and doing 'Comprehension' assignments. It brought to mind of a word that they discussed--persecution--which was new to me as a new believer. As I grow spiritually, I recognised that the word 'persecution' is frequently used in Christianity. That word left a deep impression upon me, as though preparing to accept that a true Christian's walk with Christ would not be 100% a bed of roses. There would some paths filled with thorns, but I understand then that hardships are necessary to strengthen my character so that I am prepared for whatever God has in store for me ahead.

During the discussion, everyone was so well-versed. It was around 10 p.m. and Max started to call me to ask whether I had finished my 'whatever meeting'. I remembered he used to get worried about me going home late and why Christian congregations take such a long

time to finish. He was too possessive that he called me several times to remind me to go home after 10 p.m. I wish he can join me one day to observe our activities.

Perhaps some activities do drag on more than necessary. Some working Christians do find it challenging, especially those who would prefer most meetings to be efficiently managed within a time frame. A long meeting in anytime, anywhere does exhaust anyone's spirit and will after all. But with this cell group, I find no fault with them. Why should I complain about them making me feel at home? Some fellowships are worth investing a little more time in it. Before I left, the whole group prayed for me. I felt privileged that so much attention was given to me. And that is Christian life. We pray for one another and encourage one another.

I was pretty much looking forward to joining the Cell Group meetings in Penang but I could never make it because my house is located far from my church. By the time I got back after the meeting was dismissed, it might be very late in the night. Truelight Baptist Church, the church which is at close proximity to my old house did not have Cell Group meetings at the time I joined them.

Thank God. GBC provides me everything I need in one church. It is close-by my new house. It is important for Christians to join Cell Group because anytime if a member has a problem, the Cell Group members will support. In a large church, it is impossible for the pastors to give attention to all the members. So, the Cell Group leader will take care of his sheep.

God created us to live in a community.[1]

---

1 Genesis 2:18 Man was created as a social creature "It is not good for man to be alone...".

You may be wondering why Christianity have not moved forward with the times and form discipleship via on social media sites like Facebook or Twitter? There have, in fact, and no, not to say that it is wrong to use Facebook or other social apps as tools to reach out to the lost and broken needing Jesus' touch. But there is something more real about face-to-face communication with people that social media cannot replace, and that is substantial fellowship building. There are more tangible feelings in a hug and hearing comforing words live from people who really care about you, something a digital Facebook 'like' can only do so much. Healthy support and healing is faster through this way than hiding behind social media posts.

I used to be reticent about sharing my personal life with others but now I am more open compared to before.

Some might find the Bible studies mundane, or spiritual issues at that moment are tough to digest, let alone answer. But I felt that it ultimately serves a good platform to train ourselves to have our own minds as the Holy Spirit guides us to harness knowledge and share our opinions with others. When I first joined a Cell Group, whenever I was nescience of a particular topic, I just stayed quiet. I used to think that it was better not say anything when you are unsure of what you are getting into. I used to be reticent about sharing my personal life with others but now I am more open compared to before. Sometimes, I participated in debates because I have my points of contention when a particular topic catches my attention.

In essence, Cell Group is a platform for Christians to grow together and encourage one another.

Fellowship in a cell group: Usually held in a home setting. After Bible discussion, members will have fellowship together

THE BIBLE STUDY FELLOWSHIP

I still remembered Sow Ying (Chapter 15) posted on my Facebook wall asking where the Bible Study Fellowship (BSF) is in Penang. She was kind enough to help me find a suitable Bible study group. She knew and understood the importance of spiritual growth and my need for it.

Not long after that, another Christian friend of mine gave me an invitation card for an introductory session of BSF. I was not ready to join that time. I comforted myself that BSF lessons was not scarce and is not held only in one location. There are more than 1000 classes on six continents in nearly 40 nations worldwide.

Bible study is all about us drawing us closer to God and building a stronger relationship with Him. Some may say that the Bible is generally outpaced by our modern era's evolving ways, but I beg to differ. Give it a chance, and one would see the timeless values in it that are still relevant for everyone today. What impressed me about BSF is the very organised manner of regulating thousands of people around the world--men, women and children--to assemble on the same week so that all of them could study the same Bible lesson together.

Due to the fact that I am unfamiliar with the ancient cultures, traditions, philosophies and way of speech of the people in the Bible, I must admit that my interpretation of God's word in the Bible is

lacking. It can be hard sometimes to comprehend or emphatise some of the biblical's people actions and words, and it can be harder still to figure what their stories could teach us today. Ever and again I read many times but I still do not get it. Often I have read through a verse and the next day I cannot even remember what I have perused before.

Thankfully, many are willing to share with me that through BSF, we will find new insights through discussions every week, aside from listening to the lectures or sermons.

I thought that doing daily devotion with the Lord, attending prayers meetings, Cell Group Meetings, mentoring programme, Sunday sermons, etc. was more than sufficient to keep me on my toes. Now there is another Herculean task of doing assignments for BSF. I was told that BSF is very challenging where participants are assigned with a lot of homework. At my age, I am rather wary about reliving the experience of going back to school. Already leading a fully-packed life now, doing extra activities and school assignments on the side sounded daunting and life-draining, so I held back. Whenever I was being invited to join BSF, I always gave the excuse that I was not ready and I will be more ready to go for it when I am retired.

Then again, I did not expect myself to feel inadequate. I started to feel guilty about giving constant excuses. The cravings to understand God's words more soon outgrew my excuses, hence in year 2014, I made up my mind to join BSF. It happened sooner than I thought. Well, at least I had planned to join for a year and will decide later whether I should continue subsequently. I believe God has a lot of things He wants to reveal to me, so I trust in Him that He will lead me to lessons that only He knows my heart needed it.

To find out more about BSF, visit https://www.bsfinternational. org/

Bible Study Fellowship in a group

OUR DAILY BREAD

Recalling how I came across a series of devotional mini books called 'Our Daily Bread', I remembered Ricky Soo wrote me a message in Facebook.

> Dear Winnie,
>
> Pls be sure you get a copy of Our Daily Bread. It's essential especially for a new Christian like you.
>
> 1 September 2010 16:25

I remembered telling my son one morning that I was going to have my 'Daily Bread' for breakfast. He asked me where the bread was.

I tried to explain to him--in a language that he understands-- that the 'Daily Bread' cannot be simply found on Earth, and that the bread is not for our stomachs. Like waking up in the morning everyday hungry for breakfast, we experience deep hunger within our souls. Jesus calls Himself the "bread of life". He declared in John 6:35, "I am the bread of life. He who comes to me will never go hungry, and he who believes in me will never be thirsty."

To me, "Our Daily Bread" is a hassle-and-fuss-free spiritual breakfast. In it, I enjoyed reading the inspiring stories written succintly by around 17 authors around the world. From each story, there are substantial lessons that could be drawn from the Bible verses. Everyday, there is a specific message from God for us through each of these stories. The daily devotional thoughts published in Our Daily Bread help us spend time in God's Word everyday. "As newborn babes, desire the pure milk of the Word, that you may grow thereby" (1 Peter 2:2)

Christ feeds our hungry souls just as bread feeds our bodies. One may argue that other things in life can feed our souls, aside from Christ, such as dreams, aspirations and ambitions. There is nothing wrong in enjoying the physical bread of this world that nourishes our physical bodies. But there will come a time our dreams may evolve as we grow older, wiser. Our souls will search for a fulfillment that external materialism or even some dreams could fail to make us happy. Humans are always looking for a deeper connection to these two things called 'joy' and 'perfect peace'. Today, we are bombarded by countless advertisements, trying to hammer to our consciousness that if you buy their products, you would gain prestige, wealth, fame, romance, etc. all materials that equates to happiness you think you need it, but most of the time it does not work for you.

What kind of bread on earth could soothe such fears and worries?

There will come a time our souls will start to fear about a possibly bleak future, worry about our dwindling lifeline resources or doubting about certain choices to make. What kind of bread on earth could soothe such fears and worries?

This is where we have to realise that there is no such bread in our living world that can do that, no matter how far we may travel to find such a bread. This is where we have to admit fully that we cannot do anything else but lean on Jesus. This is where we have to accept that without Jesus' daily bread unto us, we cannot go on living a good life permeated with true joy and perfect peace. But with Jesus' Word in our lives, He will satisfy our every hunger, soothe every fear and heal every wound.

This is where we have to realise that there is no such bread in our living world that can do that, no matter how far we may travel to find such a bread.

That is why in our prayer, we cite 'Give us today our daily bread' as in Matthew 6:11--it means we are acknowledging that God is our sustainer and provider, and we place our trust in God to provide what we need daily.

For more information about Our Daily Bread, visit www.odb.org To subscribe 'Our Daily Bread' visit http://odb.org/

Abba Father,
You fed me with your Word of God,
Day by night I grew and grew.
Emerging from a cocoon into a butterfly.

MY JOURNEY OF TRANSFORMATION

Before I even knew of a need to be perfect in Christ, the Lord has seen to it that I would have a source of help to bridge me closer to Him. That would explain why at one point of time, the Lord had arranged Jane to come into my life, and she became my spiritual mentor thereafter to help transform me into a 'butterfly' in the Lord's eye.

If I were to transform into a 'butterfly' on my own, it would have taken too long a time to succeed, and may achieve little success in the end. I knew that to be successful in anything, I would first need to be realistic that success is not a one-man show. I need God's favour and support from others to give me the strength that I do not possess to realise this goal. That is why fellowship with other like-minded Christians is important--they will be your keys to aid your spiritual growth with God. When you face insurmountable odds in your walk with Christ one day, your friends will pull you up to be on your feet again.

For a new believer, finding a spiritual mentor helps in spiritual growth. Not every Christian has the privilege of having spiritual mentor to guide him in his journey with Christ. So long one lifts his heart to God, asking for ways to help him grow closer to Him, keep his spiritual radar on as He will send a mentor, a guide or anything else that will help to find what one needs. I was so blessed to have one-on-one

lesson with my spiritual mentor Jane for one and a half year. We went through the Steps to Freedom in Christ, the New Believer's Kit, Discipleship and Masterlife. Although I told Jane that Pastor Lai had gone through the sinners' prayer with me to renounce my sins, to be very sure that I did not leave any sin behind, Jane went through the steps again with me from the root of my family.

The course was very thorough. I learnt a lot from Jane. Sometimes, to help me discern incomprehensible topics, Jane used real-life practical examples to teach me. The way she carried herself in such Christ-like manner in everything she does, I found myself adopting good habits from her eventually. I thought my blessing was going to end after completing Masterlife 1. But Jane offered to form a group of three to study Masterlife 2 The Disciple's Personality, we studied for more than half a year. Before I studied Masterlife 2, I thought character change is not important but I learnt that Christ also teaches us how to master our emotions.

The changes in me during the transformation process:

1. I managed to adjust my devotion time with the Lord first thing in the morning.

In the past, I always spent my leftover time with the Lord before I went to bed. This is an undisciplined spiritual habit that will affect our relationship with God the bad way. Even though my heart yearned for time with God, my body was too weary from a long day of work, hence I always gave way to my flesh's need for sleep. Now that I arrange my mornings just for the Lord, the results are refreshing every time because mornings are the best times with zero distractions. Those quiet moments are what empowered my being to embrace the day ahead for He is the Alpha and Omega (the beginning and the end).

2. Being messy was a norm. Now, being tidy is not just a good habit--it revitalise your spirit.

For the record, I was born with a silver spoon in the mouth. As a woman, I would say I am considered an untidy person. I considered myself untidy by nature because tidiness was not heavily emphasized unto me since childhood. After Jane came into my life, she taught me tips & tricks to dynamic organizational skills. What was amazing was that soon, I started to make my own bed when I wake up. I started to feel ashame of letting my maid wash my undergarments and insisted on washing myself. Besides, I wash some of my clothes. I never fathomed I would end up doing these one day, should I remain what I was in the past. Whenever I felt my energy or mind is scattered, tidying things up calms my soul. Being calm in spirit makes it easier to hear the voice of Christ and heed Him with less resistance.

3. I took on the responsibility to be good mother more seriously.

Jane had also exhorted me to be a good mother, reminding me to raise kids the right way. As her daughters are properly raised up and are very filial to her, I knew I have a lot to learn from her on parenting as she is a successful mother.

Back then, I sometimes used to despair the things that my children do. I remembered their misbehaviours and mistakes more frequently than their good deeds or achievements. On really trying days, I may have thought, "Why can't I have more submissive kids? Why can't they be like other smarter, nicer kids in their schools?" At times, my kids may have sensed this, which may have made them rebellious in retaliation. They retreated further away from me, despite my best intentions.

One day, I was given a book 'New Life Discipleship Series' to read. One of the verses that struck my attention was this,

"There is none righteous, no, NOT ONE... For ALL have sinned, and come short of the glory of God."

This was the verse that taught me to really look at myself honestly for the first time, before finding fault at my kids or at others. It was this verse that Jane exhorts me not to try to change others. "Just focus on transforming yourself," she said, "When people can really see positive transformation changes in you, they will want to know how that happened, what kind of God you have that changed you so much."

Just focus on transforming yourself...When people see the changes in you to a better person, they will want to know how that happened, what kind of God you have that changed you so much.

This advice was given to me a couple of years back. I remembered reading the first book of parenting by Gary Chapman and Ross Campbell 'The Five Love Languages of Children' and I learnt how to build up strong relationship with my children. After taking up Jane's advice and the book's parenting tips, that was where I saw visible changes in my family. I learnt to talk less and let them talk more instead. I learnt to balance better the times to be firm with my kids and when to go easy on them. By patiently emphatising with what my family members go through in their daily lives, I learnt the true meaning of trust and let go--trusting them to make the right decisions maturely, and let go more of my often-unfounded worries for them. Through this way, my kids' responses became more positive when they realised they are in the presence of a slower-to-judge adult.

Looking back now, I felt I have grown to be a better mother than I was before, thanks to Christ's insights and Jane's teachings.

4. I no longer fear the darkness–literally and figuratively-speaking. I believe everyone was afraid of the dark at some point of their lives. Some of us have outgrown it now, while some look at it with trepidation still. Darkness is an expansive mystery--some of its secrets are misunderstood, some are best left undiscovered. Darkness is not absolutely synonymous with children's bedtime monsters lurking at the corners--I am referring to spirits beyond our living world, or manifestation of our chronic negative thoughts that could become self-fulfilling prophesies. I used to fear the dark so much because deep inside, I felt insecure, weak and powerless. I was afraid that I would be unable to resist the strength of Darkness should it come upon me. Little did I know then that it is my Fears that Darkness feeds upon it. The more I fear and worry, the more those scary things I imagined it there would become seemingly more real. When Christ came in my life, I was introduced to the true Prince of Peace that shines away the darkness. That is when I knew that Christ does not abide in things that are against the grain of His holy nature. All negative or fearful thoughts do not come from the Lord. It is through His Grace that set me free from this fear of Darkness.[1]

5. Dreams were all that matters then. Now, God's will is more important.

---

[1] 2 Timothy 1:7 For the Spirit God gave us does not make us timid, but gives us power, love and self-discipline.

Dreams are powerful Life force itself. It could drive us to do things we otherwise would not normally do. Sometimes, we are beset with many ambitions or ideas, but alas, we only have limited time on Earth! One can be ambitious to excel in all dreams but the cost to fulfill it must be considered carefully.[1] For instance, when one tries to stretch himself to fulfill all his dreams, chances are high that midway, he may get burnt out and eventually abandon all dreams. Some dreams turned out to be someone else's and not yours, which would leave you wondering if that constitutes to true happiness the Lord wants for you. Some dreams are the latest fads for this season, but it may lose its glamour the next season, which would leave you a choice to continue nurturing it, or give God's dreams a chance to prevail.

In my case, I have and am living the dreams I wanted already--a marriage to a good man, a good family to be thankful for & have kids who make me feel that motherhood is worthwhile living for. But God has more for me than I ever dreamt possible. So now, whatever things I do, I commit to the Lord. I ask for God's intervention. I no longer have such strong desire to do my will first. I still do have my dreams but I will tell the Lord what I wanted to do. If it is not going well, I will ask God whether that stumbling block at that time is trying to teach me perseverance, or it is a sign from God to quit pursuing that path further. Previously, I struggled on my own for success because I relied on my own strength to do things my way. Now, I humble myself before God and am dependent on God and the Holy Spirit's guidance.

God has taken over my burden and I have faith in HIM that He will take care of everything, even my dreams.

---

1 2 Luke 14:28 (ERV) For which of you, desiring to build a tower, does not first sit down and count the cost, whether he has enough to complete it?

6. Gossip was a fun spice of life then. Now, Gossip drain precious time and our spirits, at best; Gossip could hurt & destroy someone else's life, at worst.

God has taken over my burden and I have faith in HIM that he will take care of everything, even my dreams.

It is inevitably part of human nature to gossip, that I can't and won't bother to deny. Gossiping is a sin in Christianity. The reason I gossip less is I do spend more of my time with the Lord, in Bible studies and the church which leaves me very little time to gossip. For those who have the wrong impression that church people get together to gossip about others, I would like to share what we talk about with our fellow brethen in Christ. Most of the time, the conversation topics are about God and Bible studies. We do not even talk about our businesses or professions in church. If we do fellowship, some of the healthy conversation topics we talk about are travelling, food, sick people--the progress and update of our prayer for God's healing according to His will.

About Gossip, depending on the nature of a conversation's flow, gossips can--ironically--reveal theories & axioms about life, love, human nature and more for us to ponder on. But how we respond to Gossip makes the difference. Since Christ came into my life, the Holy Spirit had prompted me to distance myself more from the powerful pull of Gossip. I have learnt that Gossip could easily steer our minds to judge someone unjustly. More often than not, Gossip has a negative energy that could limit a person's progress to change.

Even though Gossip provides good opening lines & fodder when we socialise, Gossip can become a powerful sin that could destroy

someone. Hence, I am learning to refrain from this sin. One thing I find found interesting that Jane did was she stuck a note on her computer screen, which read "Ephesians 4:29 Do not let any unwholesome talk come out of your mouths, but only what is helpful for building others up according to their needs, that it may benefit those who listen."

7. Doing charity quietly is more sincere than publicised charity.

I have to admit that I still do publicised charity work when organising community events. It is inevitable that for these type of events, we need to give recognition to the sponsors.

Doing charity works requires certain degree of limelight, depending how-highly publicised the charity functions are. For instance, an orphanage may draw attention to not the orphans' plight first but to the VIP supporting the orphans. A powerful patron can boost a charity's house prestige and popularity tremendously, not to mention the funds needed to continue providing for the charity's cause. Now, I do not mind these superior elites lending their names to charities. What God had taught me so far is that their hearts' intentions matter more to Him than just their outward looks and actions.[1]

Admit it, people knew inherently how to look good before others. Some of them are experts at hiding their skeletons in the closets well. It would hurt God equally and as much as I would be if, -- for example-- a celebrity known for his generosity at charities is actually a selfish miser with his own biological family behind the scenes.

---

1 2 Luke 15:14-15 The Pharisees, who were lovers of money, heard all these things, and they ridiculed him (Jesus). 15 And he (Jesus) said to them, "You are those who justify yourselves before men, but God knows your hearts. For what is exalted among men is an abomination in the sight of God.

The publicised community work that I do is more about my passion to do it. I take it as in Matthew 5:16 In the same way, let your light so shine before men, that they may see your good works and glorify your Father in Heaven. This is how I would be answerable to God.

On the other hand, God is teaching me to do charity quietly. God has not asked me to judge the rich or poor; I have better worries to be mindful about, such as about my own attitude when it comes to giving and seeing to the needs of the needy. This is something we are all answerable to God. Because when no man is watching and expecting standards from you that time, your true goodwill grows when doing charity quietly. With only God watching you, and He sees your heart's sincerity and that is when He would reward you in due time.[1]

Because when no man is watching and expecting standards from you that time, your true goodwill grows when doing charity quietly.

8. I have learnt to care for others beyond myself or family needs

There are times when we cannot do much physical work for the poor, needy and lost. Distance, time, low spiritual strength level in Christ and/or other financial commitments could play factors to that. personal needs or family's well-being, which I thought was good enough. I was not concerned for strangers beyond my immediate contacts. What changed my perspective on this was this verse--Luke

[1] Matthew 6 3-4 3 But when you give to the needy, do not let your left hand know what your right hand is doing. 4 so that your giving may be in secret. Then your Father, who sees what is done in secret, will reward you.

6:34-36.[1] It did not go down well with me initially, but its truth was necessary to extend my outlook of compassion for others.

From this verse, that was how I became less self-centred and started to challenge myself to pray for people that I do not know. Even if there were irksome enemies in my waking hour, I kept reminding myself that they have a purpose in life under God's will. For all I know, they could be in my life to teach me about patient love God wanted to etch into my character. Christians who could pray for their enemies tend to have a broader heart and vision to pray for nations, governments and worldwide humanity issues. They knew ahead that some of these current issues may someday affect us in the long-term. Take for instance, the 2013 national elections in Malaysia. In the past, I never bothered to participate in an election polls before. Racial and religious harmony here was sacrosanct. After I came to know Christ, I became more aware of the diatribes levelled at the arguably weak governance of my country. This consequently awakened my realisation that just praying for my nation was not going to be enough.

In the past, I never bothered to participate in an election polls before. Racial and religious harmony here was sacrosanct.

Prayer-warrior Christians take these issues more seriously during corporate prayer meetings regularly. Some Christians and I have become more pro-active about the vision of change. So I decided to

---

[1] Luke 6:34-36 "If you lend to those from whom you expect to receive, what credit is that to you? Even sinners lend to sinners in order to receive back the same amount. 35 "But love your enemies, and do good, and lend, expecting nothing in return; and your reward will be great, and you will be sons of the Most High; for He Himself is kind to ungrateful and evil men. 36 "Be merciful, just as your Father is merciful.

participate in the Election poll to exercise my right to vote for our country in 2013.

In other words, knowing Christ would leave Apathy little to no room in our lives. Jesus' true disciples would actualise the true meaning of caring for one another in reality, be it through prayer, or proactive action.

9. Life becomes richer when your friendship circle expands.

One day, maybe when you realised you are imprisoned too long in a never-ending rat race, you would be asking yourself, "Is this all there is to life? Why am I still not happy, even though I have all the (material) riches that I wanted?" Or during a medical check-up when your doctor announces, "You have only few months/years to live if you don't do something about your health," we would question ourselves what is our true calling in life we have overlooked all this time. As a result, we would go on a spiritual journey to find ourselves after that. In that journey of self-discovery, we may realised that the secret to live our life purpose fully is not in the quantity of friends we have, but in the quality of our relationships with people and with ourselves.

Some of you may have too many friends in your contact list. So understandably, you may have wondered how many are your true friends you can count on during a crisis? Some of us have not gone out so much that our circle of friends is miserably small. Since I have found my life purpose in Christ, I found peace with myself after living long years in fear and seclusion. With that newfound confidence, I managed to make more Christian friends. My friends circle has increased multiple-fold ever since. Because my friends and I found the same purpose in Christ, I felt as if I am living in a large family with many brothers and sisters, blessed to have a rich, fulfilling relationship with each of them.

10. My English proficiency has improved.

Before that, I naïvely thought my English standard was good enough for me to aspire to become an English teacher. But the more I mingle with Christians, I realised that I had a lot to catch up with the Christians who generally have a better command in English. I do not deny that there are some Malaysian Christian groups out there who prefer their church services to be conducted in their local mother-tongue dialects. But with this Christian group I chose to be with, I made myself learnt a lot of Christianese[1] and jargons from the Bible. By observing the mature Christians in the English church services, I made the effort to re-learn the English grammar, vocabulary and sentence structures more seriously so that my articulation of the English language becomes stronger in due time.

But with this Christian group I chose to be with, I made myself learnt a lot of Christianese and jargons from the Bible.

Would Life be more smooth-sailing if one accepts Jesus into their lives? I am sorry to burst the bubble but no, Life will still throw at you storms, thorns and muck along the way. Besides, we cannot ignore the fact that there is a cost to be Jesus' disciples. That cost requires us Christians to consider carefully if we can truly give up the ways of the world we are so used to --a.k.a. carry our cross--and follow Jesus' way of things thoroughly.[2]

---

1 Christianese- A language used by Christians with terms, catchphrases and theological and influenced by popular translations of the Bible.

2 Luke 14:27 Whoever does not bear his own cross and come after me cannot be my disciple.

So yes, I would say a Christian life & following Jesus is no bed of roses all the way. But you will have some moments of respite, because Life is not made of one season only. Such is the cycle of Life where Change is constant, each season bringing us different things in different times.[1]

When a season of Trials dawn on any of us, of course Trials would be intimidating. We are fearful of Trials because of we fear the high possibility of failure and unable to endure the pain that comes from failure. But to look at the other side of the coin here, Trials & Failures are Life's better teachers than Blessings sometimes. When Life sails by too smoothly, we have a tendency to take God for granted. For my case, I may find myself distancing away from Him and become deeply-absorbed with my worldly responsibilities and obligations. That is why when times of difficulty do come upon me, I look at it as opportunities to cling to Jesus more.[2]

11. I am going back to schooling time.

---

[1] Ecclesiastes 3
1 For everything there is a season, and a time for every matter under heaven:

3a time to kill, and a time to heal;
a time to break down, and a time to build up;

4 a time to weep, and a time to laugh;
a time to mourn, and a time to dance;

6a time to seek, and a time to lose,
a time to keep, and a time to cast away;

8a time to love, and a time to hate;
a time for war, and a time for peace.

[2] Psalm 119:71 The suffering You sent was good for me,
for it taught me to pay attention to Your principles

I have never expected myself going back to studies until after I have become a Christian. Attending sermons is like attending lectures. In my daily life, I read Scripture from the Bible, Our Daily Bread, Christian books, etc. Christian life is all about reading and feeding ourselves with the Word of God. If I am lazy to read, I will switch on my Audio Bible and listen.

12. I learn how to keep a spiritual journal to record the scriptures and summary of sermon points that inspire me.

13. Life is more disciplined.

Everyday when I wake up, I do my daily devotion and before I sleep I pray. He is the Alpha and Omega (the beginning and the end). So I spend time with the Lord early in the morning and before I go to bed. During the day, I pray before I eat. I commit my daily activities to the Lord through short prayers. Before I go to bed, I usually count my blessings of the day by giving thanks to the Lord.

I might be backslided in life but this will be a blueprint for me in my Christian life.

Have I really been one hundred per cent transformed and being perfected after accepting the Lord? The answer is a firm 'NO'. Although I have ameliorated myself as a person, I am still not one hundred per cent perfect like the saint. I am still in a work-in-progress and it will be a life-long journey. I can only claim that I have been transformed to be a child of God which enables me to inherit the Kingdom of God. I am still living in my sinful flesh but when I desire the Holy Spirit's guidance, I am able to live a righteous life. Till today, I still am asking God to continue to mould me to be like His son Jesus.[1]

---

[1] Psalm 73:26 "My flesh and my heart may fail, but God is the strength of my heart and my portion forever."

We should change to be like little children, humble and be dependent on God with our sincere hearts. Then only we can inherit the kingdom of heaven.[1]

Poem:

Transformation- Crying Soul

-Winnie L.B.Toh

My soul cries out to You Oh Lord, "I am not perfect and I am not the saint."
Give me the desire to follow Your footprints
Here I am for you to paint!
Mould me and guide me, to set my blueprint.

My soul cries out to You Oh Lord, "Where is the fruit of Your spirit on my tree?"
In the stillness, His voice consoles
Love, Joy, Peace,.. He gave these for free
And He whispers to me, "Be Faithful, Be Gentle and have Self-control."

Patience, Kindness and Goodness will slowly grow
But Lord Oh Lord! I am a sinner, I am flawed
The Lord reminds me His words below

---

[1] Matthew 18:3 "Truly I tell you, unless you change and become like little children, you will never enter the kingdom of heaven."

Let the Holy word dwell in you and follow My law.

I nail my sinful nature to the cross
And will pray pray pray when I go astray
Forgive me Oh Father when I make you crossed
You gave me many saving graces that I can't repay.

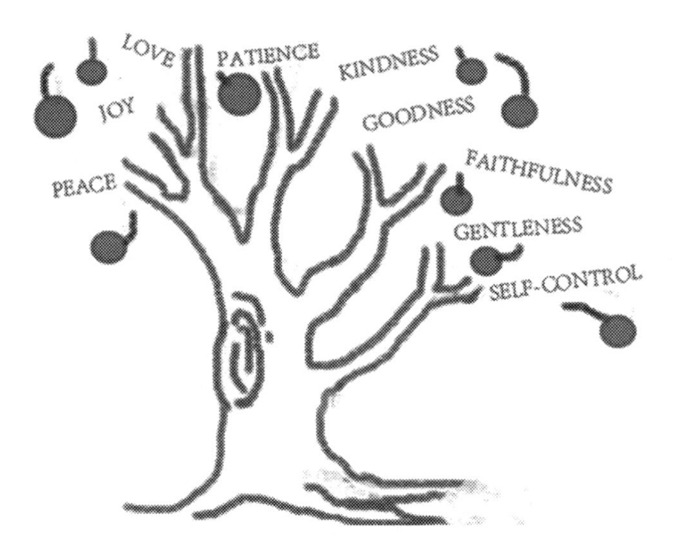

Galatians 5:22-23

But the fruit of the Spirit is love, joy, peace, patience, kindness, goodness, faithfulness, gentleness and self-control. Against such things there is no law.

If you ever wonder what a true Christian is supposed to be like, do refer to the 'Fruit of the Spirit' model. It is the blueprint for a Christian's character. But it seems impossible to work for all the nine traits

listed. However, as we grow in Christ, the Holy Spirit will dwell in us and help us to be better individuals. The Holy Spirit will guide each of us to know and adhere to Jesus' moral standards for us-–to love our enemies, to forgive others and reconcile immediately, do not slander others, etc. The list of 'don't-commit-these-sins' can be found in Galataians 5:19-21, among them are sexual immorality, impurity and debauchery; idolatry and witchcraft; hatred, discord, jealousy, fits of rage, selfish ambition, dissensions, factions and envy; drunkenness, orgies, and the like.

Before I knew Christ, I always thought that I was perfect. After learning of God's standards in the 'Fruit of the Spirit' model, I think I deserve to go to Hell. Sometimes, I wondered why did I accept Christ if His standards are onerous, to begin with. Why had I chosen a difficult God to worship when for even one small sin that I commit, it is still a sin in God's eye? To Him, no one can achieve His standard of righteousness. I reiterate this verse stated previously:

ROMANS 3:10, 23

'There is none righteous, no, NOT ONE... For ALL have sinned, and come short of the glory of God.'

At the end of the day, God knew that we cannot do it on our own. We all have to be humble enough to admit that our own strengths are not going to get us far with God's decrees. That was why Jesus came to this world to pay for the penalty for our sins by dying on the cross.[1] It was this verse that gave me an unshakeable sense of peace that things will turned out alright in the end because I have an almighty God who will see to it that I am made righteous in His sight.

---

[1] *John 3:16 For God so loved the world that he gave his one and only Son, that whoever believes in him shall not perish but have eternal life.*

THE GOOD NEWS

Before I became a Christian, I always wondered why Christians have that sense of urgency to convert as many people as possible to Christianity. Now I know the answer: they loved us enough to not want us perished.

By right, we are all sinners at some point in time. You may have never physically point a knife at someone's throat and thrust that blade into his throat, but think about other sins you think that was not a big deal then. How about the time you lied to your parents to save yourselves from trouble? What about back-stabbing your sibling who had always shared his meals with you? Or maybe you had once coveted for your best friend's girlfriend? How many couples have sex before marriage when in the God's eye, the bride is suppose to walk down the aisle virgin pure? You get the pattern here--all these sins lead to guilt. Guilt will haunt you of that sin you committed. The more you feed on this guilt, the more that guilt will remind you that you do not deserve to live again because of your sin that seems unpardonable. Sin leads us to Hell.

You realised that you decide do something about that sin haunting your sleep and waking moments. What can we do about it? Hear the 'Good News' I'm about to tell you now, because this 'Good News' is the truth that will set you free.

What is 'Good News'? What do the Christians mean by 'Good News'? I used to hear it before I converted. But I did not know the exact meaning of it.

The 'Good News' means that Christ has died for our sins and rose again from the dead to be our living Savior.

I used to think that Christianity is just a religion. But now I know that it is more about the way of living life in Christ-like manner, it is about a personal relationship with God. So after the transformation, I have a hugely different perspective on Christian- ity. It does not emphasise on good morals or good deeds to gain our salvation. It is more about our faith in Christ and our living relationship with him. Salvation is given FREE to anyone who accepts Christ as personal Saviour. It is the gift of God. This is the Good News and it is up to people to choose to accept HIM.

I have been set free by the Lord and now I can fly high

The caterpillar must die and go into a cocoon. Then the transformation only takes place to become a butterfly.

THE TREMOR

On 11 April 2012, I was sitting in front of my laptop, awaiting inspiration from the Holy Spirit for this last chapter of my book. I could be sharing another testimony of how beautiful my new lease of life is today because of Christ's redemption. But I do not want my readers to close this book and settle for a false impression that Life in Christ meant living a strife-free paradise.

As I was thinking along those lines, suddenly, I felt the earth trembled beneath me. I was seated on the third floor of my house when I felt the vibration. The loud sound of the window glasses shaking made my head reeled in giddiness. My mind began to reel. What could have triggered the tremor? Was this landslide or earthquake?

While half of my mind was trying to take in the tremor, half of my mind went duly blank. My body proceeded into survival action mode ahead of my dumbfounded mind--I walked down the staircase, albeit with trepidation, to my room to get my belongings. I felt my legs were shaking so much that I could barely run. I was not properly dressed up and was heading towards my wardrobe to dress up. Trembling with fear, I simply grabbed a pyjamas top to wear with jeans.

Minutes later, I commanded everyone to evacuate our house. None of my neighbours came out, though. I became even more confused.

Was it just my house that was shaking? Or did the whole Penang Island felt the tremor too? Why didn't anyone run out of his house, at least? I could not tell based on my neighbours because they are not at home during day time. I immediately thought of my mother at that moment and called to check whether she had felt any earthquake tremors too. Through her and from Facebook, I found out eventually from other people's stories that everyone did experience the tremor too. That tremor was the result of an 8.7 magnitude earthquake originating from Acheh, Indonesia.

I was worried if my beautiful life would end without the house. Would we be homeless and had to start all over from scratch?

There was a second tremor--a milder one--a few hours after the first one. Not long after, I heard there was a Tsunami threat in Penang. Everyone was advised to stay alert at 9 p.m. I remembered my virtual friend in Facebook asking me to prepare a torch light and stay on the topmost floor of the house, should the Tsunami strike our island's shores. He had packed up his passport and a bag filled with emergency supplies to prepare for the worst.

For the first time in my life, I was worried about the potential power of Mother Nature and how much we are at the mercy of Her moods. Geologists has found that the tectonic plates beneath our seas has shifted, making Malaysia now more vulnerable to seismic hazards resulting from the prevalence of South-East Asia geodynamic activities. If the tremor had been a bit more powerful to truly wreck our island apart, my family and I may have ended up with more than just being homeless. Would we die that hour, or survive to see another day? If the disaster had happened and we survived it, how do we start all over from scratch? Could we cope with the emotional trauma that comes from losing our once-secured home?

The tremors, the Tsunami warnings, those natural-disaster potentials that kept us all on our toes, it made me recognise despairingly that nothing is permanent in this world. When facing the prospects of Death, one tends to hark back to his past. More often than not, regrets and promises to do good hereafter would spurt out of our mouths in wake of pending Doomsday. I am no different--I regretted for not spending enough time doing the Lord's work. Even though the last Tsunami warning was a false signal, I remembered writing this on my Facebook wall:

> Life is transient, meaningless and passing. But if I have invested my time wisely in the Lord during lifetime, I have no fear of what is to come.

I remembered having a chat with my virtual friend and we joked about never able to meet up at the same place in the afterlife because he is a Buddhist and I am a Christian. The subject between us was meant to be light-hearted then, but if one takes the time to think about it, the 'Afterlife' topic is something serious to consider. The possibilities of the afterlife alerted me to ponder over a few things:

1. The gate to Heaven is narrow and the road to Hell is wide. Am I qualified to enter the narrow gate anytime from now?

Matthew 7:13 "Enter through the narrow gate. For wide is the gate and broad is the road that leads to destruction, and many enter through it."

2. We are only stewards of our children, properties, money, etc. It is easier to say than actually do what we preach that we will not be attached to anything in this world when the End Time comes.

3. Have I done enough of God's work according to His will?

Enough for Him to acknowledge me one day?

Matthew 25:21 'Well done, good and faithful servant!"

4. Have I lived my life to the fullest?

5. Every Christian is an ambassador of Christ. Have I live up to the standards of a good role model?

6. Have I said & done enough Thanksgiving unto God for His blessings in my daily life?

7. Have I done enough great work in this world to be remembered by others?

8. Have I treated my mum well during lifetime?

9. Have I done enough to be a good daughter, wife and mother to my family?

10. By publishing this book, I am subjecting myself to the scrutiny of the world as this book is my living testimony of how Christ changed every area of my life. The question is, can I keep up with the new life Christ has set for me? Can I meet expectations while maintaining His standards?

Luke 12:48

Everyone to whom much was given, of him much will be required, and from him to whom they entrusted much, they will demand the more.

If you have been accessing your life from time to time, you may have known immediately through these questions what remaining kinks in your life to sort out next. But there are many of us who may take longer to answer these. Each of these ten questions I posed seems weighty, and it is not like we take the time to stop and meditate on it frequently. Understandably, some of you may choose to brush it aside for now, because you may not be ready to evaluate it objectively.

As for me, the answer to those ten questions is admittedly, depressing—-it is a 'No' to all of them. Really, no kidding! As mentioned earlier in the previous chapter, I am a work-in-progress sinner trying to be as righteous I can be in the Lord's sight. It is not easy to be perfect, but our God is a gracious God. Just read from the beginning of Genesis until Malachi in the Bible and you would find God akin to an incredibly patient lover who loves us still despite our fallible tendencies. He loves us still despite what we were in the dark past and what we had become now. God is waiting for us to come to repentance, and wipe our sinful slates clean.

Psalm 25

8 Good and upright is the LORD; therefore he instructs sinners in the way

9 He leads the humble in what is right, and teaches the humble his way.

Psalm 36

7 How precious is your steadfast love, O God! The children of mankind take refuge in the shadow of your wings.

9 For with you is the fountain of life; in your light do we see light.

Some of you may think that there is still Time ahead because we are still considered young. Besides, it is morbid to think of death when we are still alive and kicking. But to put it in another perspective, to think of Death now can push you all the more to go after every dream you dreamt of doing, and do everything God has commanded you. Because neither you or I want to go to our death beds filled with regrets, saying 'sorry' to God for the hundredth time about things you did not finished doing, or putting to rest broken relationships you have not resolved while we had our youth then.

Before we leave this world, with our last breathe, remember to ask for forgiveness from the Lord for all our sins committed consciously or not in our lifetime. Even though we may feel that we do not have a chance, our Godly Father will forgive His children unconditionally. I may have not been that close to Death yet, but I strongly believe that when we ask for God's forgiveness, we would at least find a small measure of peace hovering at our deathbeds. That peace (however big or small it may be) is the result of our faith in Jesus Christ and the salvation He brings unto us.

Last but not least, I would like to thank the Lord Jesus for being my personal saviour. My testimonial has proven that the victory of my spiritual battle belongs to the Lord.[1] Thank You for Your promise that You are always with me until the end of the world!

---

[1] The horse is made ready for the day of battle, but victory rests with the Lord.

Poetry interspersed with the story

From a Caterpillar into a Butterfly

-Winnie L.B.Toh

I was once a caterpillar,
A pupa hiding in the cocoon before,
Comfort zone was my snug, little pillar,
There was nothing more to ask for.

A different morning is soon rising,
Extraordinary change is at nigh,
To flee from my fears is hard striving,
Shed my old skin off I did, so has Death thereby.

To see the Lord, my eyes began to open wide,
Dear Abba Father, I realise today,
All the pains that I had achingly abide,
None is like Your death at Calvary for us that day.

Like a fallen angel, I surrendered to You my spirit,
O Lord, it's You and only You I laud,
A paradigm shift coming into my life so vivid,
A New Creation in Christ, Praise God!

You deliver me from warfare with your Word,
By your Word, I grew and grew, day and night,
From a cocoon into a butterfly I emerged,
I flapped my wings to flight.

I found my poor fragile wings cut, oh no!
To the Lord, I cried out (Psalm 22) in anguish,
"Why are You so far from saving my soul,
Oh Lord! Don't forsake me here to languish

Day and night, I cried to God many a tear,
"Father, come mend my broken wings."
He sent His servants to deliver me with care,
He gives me many a reason to sing.

Sing praises to the Redeemer, I am set free!
My wings unfold and I see golden tincture,
Fly to the rainbow, fly to the sky with glee!
It's a beautiful Monarch flying, a perfect picture.

Here I am in the breeze dancing merrily,
Fluttering around with abandon near the sea,
While sipping a sweet flower's dew verily,
"You're my perfect plan," whispered the
Lord to me.

Oh Lord, indeed I am your new creation!
A butterfly now that sees wide & fly far,
For all days, from flower to flower with excitation,
I will bear You the sweetest nectar, my ethereal star.

Teach me to be a light of the world, salt of the earth,
To become what the Lord intends me to be, I'll foster.
Reveling in God's magnificent glory will be my mirth,
And all men shall praise you, Heaven
Father!

Printed in the United States
By Bookmasters